ManTracks

A Rite of Passage Program
for Christian Men

Ellis Hackler

WinePress Publishing
MUKILTEO, WA 98275

Published by WinePress Publishing
PO Box 1406
Mukilteo, WA 98275

Cover by **DENHAM**DESIGN, Everett, WA
Photos by Charles A. Dean

Printed in the United States of America.

Library of Congress Catalog Card Number: 96-61874
ISBN 1-883893-92-5

ManTracks

This book is dedicated to

my three sons:

Raymond Ellis Hackler, James Ray Benton, Jr.,
and Donald Mark Neace—boys who became men
on my watch. Tender memories in my heart, tough men
in the world—arrows from my quiver, flying farther
than I will ever go.

Table of Contents

PART III
THE MANTRACKS CEREMONY

Acknowledgments

ManTracks could never have evolved through the myriad of changes without the help and encouragement of many people. I want to acknowledge some of the helpful people who have supported the development of this work over twenty years.

My three sons made this program possible. Raymond, my only biological son, and my two step-sons, Jim and Mark were all a delight to be a dad for. Each son became my guinea pig over several years of trying different father-son programs. Each of them in turn was co-operative and enthusiastic about his own rite-of-passage program. They each have been a joy to know as sons, and they are each my good friends today as well as my protégés in the art of manhood.

I met the Cooper family, of Irving, Texas when my rite-of-passage program was only an idea. Over several years my family gradually became a part of their extended family. Participating in their family rituals through two generations significantly enhanced my definition of 'family.' Their informal rites-of-passage were the foundation for some of the ManTracks milestones. I will be forever grateful for the love and acceptance of this large family group.

Ralph and Sandra Logan saw the value in the original "Pai-Charis" program and helped me bring our son Ray into adulthood. Their cooperative spirit made Ray's rite-of-passage a meaningful reality.

Rev. Michael Lee helped me categorize countless hours of research on rites-of-passage and the biblical basis for such programs. He helped create the name "Pai-Charis" and helped me conduct the pilot program.

Thanks to John Littau, who continually insisted that "Pai-Charis" [now, ManTracks] be in print. John was responsible for organizing and managing our latest "living Lab" of godly fathers and sons.

Thanks to my friend Hal Henson, whose prayer support has sustained me through the latest version. Thanks also to my *Promise Keepers®* group: Dave Plemons, Dave Waters, Ralph Spalding, Robert Cooper and Steve Johnson. These guys kept after me until I got the task completed.

I am indebted to Laura Gschwend, Professor of Communications at Western Seminary, whose creative teaching style and personal encouragement gave me the emotional fuel I needed to complete this latest revision.

Dr. David Eckman, Professor of Hebrew and Vice President of Western Seminary's Department of Church Health has been a constant source of encouragement as he has demonstrated these principles with students and faculty at Western Seminary in San Jose, California.

Finally, and most important of all, I thank God for Deanna, my loving wife who has been my most valuable critic. From the first Pai-Charis to the present ManTracks, Deanna has been my faithful resource, my best friend, and a model mom for all our coming-of-age men.

What is this Book About?

Manhood...

When does it happen?

When does a boy become a man? (Everyone seems to know when he is not one.) It certainly is not when he can father a child—millions of abandoned children will attest to that. Nor is it when he can palm a basketball, or drive a car. Yes, we know when a boy is NOT a man, but the problem is we do not know when he is one!

The missing ingredient in the Christian community is a coming-of-age ceremony. The lack of a specific rite-of-passage from youth into adulthood has created confusion and doubt in the minds of both youth and adults. Now there is help. The instructions in this book will help fathers and sons work together on a simple but specific "Becoming a man of God" program. The major purpose of The ManTracks Program is to set the stage for The ManTracks Ceremony. The ceremony will register a point in time when the most important figure in a young person's life—his dad, publicly pronounces that he is passing from "boy" to "man."

The Christian community is unique (at least it ought to be!). Christians ought to be different than the world in the way we prepare our men folk for adulthood because we should be emphasizing different things. Unfortunately, that has not been the case over the last few years. Young men have been getting their clues from the neighborhood streets and the public school instead of the Fellowship of Saints. It is time for a change. Using the ManTracks program, fathers and sons will have tracks to follow that point men toward important, specific characteristics of male adulthood from a Christian perspective.

I first began to consider a rite of passage program when my oldest son was entering his teens. I was aware, as most men are, that these confusing years can be intensified by the ambiguity of not knowing when manhood would arrive. I read everything I could find about coming of age, and frankly there was very little information available when I began my research. Lacking direction or formal information, I simply designed my own program, producing the first ManTracks in August of 1975. I repeated the program for each of my other two sons, updating and improving it each time. Nearly twenty years later, all three of my sons testify that the ManTracks program made a dramatic and significant impact on their lives. They agree that the memory of that special day continues to give them a balanced sense of belonging and self-reliance.

ManTracks, formerly named "Pai-Charis," (a Greek term for "Son of Grace") has been tried and proven over more than twenty years. It has worked for other father-son teams and it will work for you. The important thing is not what you learn in this study guide, the important thing is that you accept the challenges in the book as two men, a father and a son, working on a project together. Keep the appointments with each other, and do the journalizing assignments. Like anything else, you will get from ManTracks what you invest into it. However, unlike any other process I know, this program will provide a pattern for you to follow that will result in an unprecedented bonding experience. And that is what the program is about.

After every chapter there are questions designed to get you to reflect on the material and communicate as father and son. I suggest that both you get a notebook to keep a personal journal of notes that you want to discuss. In Part

II, you are encouraged to develop an album from pictures, letters to each other, and other memoirs you gather as you work your way through ManTracks. Other father-son teams who have completed this program have displayed this "Digest" at the reception following their rite of passage ceremony, and later placed it among their family heirlooms. More about that later. The point is that ManTracks is more than a book to read. It is a relationship-building tool, a way to keep track of the interaction every son needs and every father wishes he had received from his dad.

A Brief Word About Writing ...

I have encountered a few men who balk at the ManTracks program because they feel they can't write very well. Some guys have difficulty expressing themselves, especially on paper. That's not because they are incapable of it. It is because, in many cases, they have not been given a lot of opportunity to do it. Many fellows grow up being trained that it is unmanly to express feelings and writing in journals is sissy stuff. Something is drastically wrong with this picture. Consider one of the most famous Bible characters of all time, King David. The Bible calls him a man after God's own heart. Was he a sissy? If you lived in his kingdom and valued your life, you would never have called him a wimp! David's personal journals —we call them the Psalms— certainly did not nullify his masculinity. How about Peter, our Lord's boisterous disciple? Now there is a man's man! Yet, no greater prose can be found in all of literature than his two books in the New Testament. Remember, he was an unlearned fisherman, a guy with sun-tanned face and fish-smelling hands—not a mamma's boy with a graduate degree in poetic journalism.

So go ahead, practice your God-given right to self-expression. This is one program where real men write. Don't worry about grammar, or getting the right words, or even getting the words right. That is not what this is about. This is about being honest and truthful to someone you really love. After you have written your ideas, get alone together as father and son to discuss your thoughts. Practice really listening to one another. And by the way dad, don't do all the talking. Son, take advantage of this situation to show respect. Really talk to one another. Ask questions and worry less about answers than putting words to your relationship. This is something you both want, and you both know it. So lets get to it!

PART I

A Mandate for Men

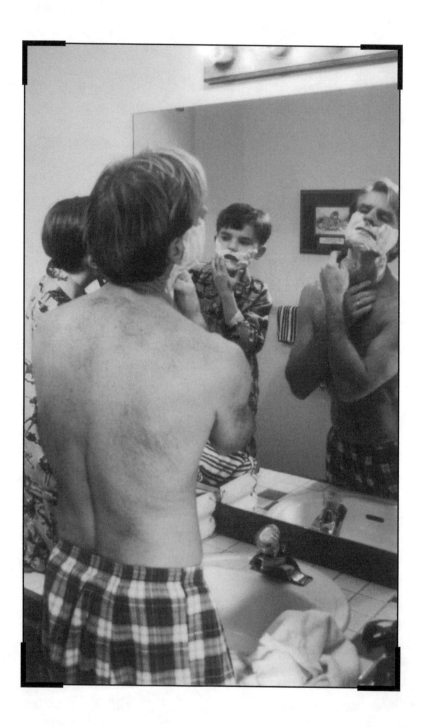

CHAPTER 1

THE WAKE-UP CALL

Jim, my oldest son, came to the doorway of my bedroom where I was sitting at my desk, working on something not nearly as important as what he was about to say. Leaning against the doorjamb as if it would fall, hands jammed deeply into his pockets, he had that familiar posture. This always signaled a pow wow. I usually read the signal and initiated the conversation. But this time he broke the silence first. "Dad," he began, lowering his voice as deeply as possible, "could I borrow your razor...?"

It wasn't like I was blind. I had seen a little fuzz on his chin, between the pimples, but I had unconsciously avoided the issue. He was, after all, only fourteen. When I was fourteen, I was asking my dad for the car keys. Jim was asking me for a razor. I was getting a wake-up call!

Jim needed more from me than a razor, and we both knew it. He was becoming a man and he needed to know that I was aware of what was going on inside him—not just what was growing on his chin. Because I had been alone through my turbulent teen years, my unthinking emotions had ignored the signs that Jim was coming of age. I wasn't ready for this! But ready or not his manhood was fast approaching, and I wanted us to experience it together. The next few years would be hard on Jim, and I did not want him to experience the anxiety I knew as a teenager. Jim would need guidance through the thousand yawning pitfalls waiting to devour budding men. How could I help him become a man when I was not sure how myself? So I did what every God-fearing father does under these circumstances: I quietly panicked!

He covered the distance from his leaning post to my bathroom shaving station in two or three steps, although I realized that he had been making the journey for about ten years. I watched him standing there, looking so tall and grown up. Our eyes met momentarily as he picked up the razor and the pack of blades, holding them in his hands just the way I do it.

"Are you sure you know how to use that thing?" I asked, with nervous humor that was way too obvious. This seemed like uncharted ground for both of us, but it really wasn't. He had never shaved before, but he had watched me do it hundreds of times. That's how we learn, by watching dad to it.

"I think so," he grinned, taking the Schick Injector® from my hand. "But if you want, you can give me a few pointers." He seemed to understand my fatherly concern. I reached up and touched his jaw with the back of my hand, gently feeling the infant whiskers. The emotions going on inside me were unexplainable. This is man stuff. It didn't need verbalizing.

"I'll help you," my voice almost cracked from the emotion—but, being a man, I didn't want to let it show. I cleared my throat and continued, "You can do it…" That's what every lad needs. Not a week-end seminar on how-to's, just an available dad, with a simple, "I'm here."

"I'll show you…"

"We'll do it together…"

As I reflect on that experience, I know it was a turning point in Jim, and in me. We stepped over a threshold together during the precious fleeting seconds it took for the shaving cream to gush into a ball in his hand. Maybe I'm too sentimental, but I think a simple thing like a young man's first shave can be a big deal. If handled correctly by dad, it can be a rite of passage. Like learning to drive, or going on the first date. We don't have to go to the woods and smoke silly-putty to establish a passage. Little things can mark a moment in time when the lad steps over a never-to-be-repeated threshold. There is a moment in every young adult's life when they make that passage. Problem is, not everyone is ready when the time comes. Often, men miss the entire process and never even know what they missed. Like me. No one was there to help me recognize the moment and capture it. I wasn't about to let that happen to Jim.

But just knowing that young men need a guide into manhood isn't enough. We need to do something about it. I think we need a ceremony to celebrate the manhood passage, and I know I am not alone. Three eminent Christian psychologists who are virtual icons of Spiritual leadership in the company of saints today are Dr. Frank Minirth (of the famed Minirth Meier New Life Clinics), Dr. Brian Newman, and Dr. Paul Warren. In their book, *Fathers, An Instruction Manual*, they say:

"It's true, there is no rite of passage in the church as a whole for kids entering adolescence. Some denominations have confirmation, for instance, but not universally.

19

So they create a youth group because they don't know what else to do with you. There needs to be an event run by fathers as a rite of passage. Something recognized by everyone, like a barmitzvah. In the family and also in the Spiritual family, the church."[1]

People obviously need ceremony. Every society has culture-bound methods to punctuate their existence, celebrating their passage through important events. Weddings and graduations are by far the most common examples in America, but there are also many others. Wherever you go you can see pictures, plaques, and trophies, prominently posted in mute evidence of what we value. The missing ingredient in the Christian community is a coming-of-age ceremony. The lack of a specific rite-of-passage from youth into adulthood has left a cauldron of confusion for both youth and adults in contemporary America. It was certainly true of me. I had no idea when (or if) my passage into manhood occurred. Certainly it wasn't the hair on my chin or anywhere else on my body that made me a man. I wanted desperately to do something about this dilemma for Jim and my other two sons.

A few days earlier I had been flipping through a Christian magazine when I came across a one-page article telling how one man had created a "Christian Bar-Mitzvah" for his son. It fueled an idea that this razor incident was about ignite. I had to do something like that for Jim.

That was the beginning of ManTracks. When I first started this program, it didn't know what to name it. Maybe it was my marketing background, but I wanted a name that would identify what this rite of passage program was all about. I wanted it to be one word, or a short title, but masculine adulthood has a very illusive definition. It means something slightly different in every culture, and it even differs from generation to generation within cultures. It is a hard concept to grasp, and harder to hold on to. Since most men don't have a clue how to define or describe the state of arrival into manhood, it is no surprise that we have a hard time getting there. It's like asking someone where they are going and hearing them say, "I don't know, but I have to hurry because I am late." Christian maturity, on the other hand, is an easier definition to grasp because there are character guidelines in the Bible that describe godliness. That's why I use the Bible so extensively in the ManTracks program. It seems to me that since God made us, it would save us a lot of heartache if we would consult the manufacturer's operator's manual once in a while.

The product you have before you is the result of many years of trial and error, but that first program was quite an adventure! Jim and I had a lot of fun designing the program together from scratch. We started at ground zero. I read everything I could find about coming of age, and there was pitifully little information available when I began my research. Lacking direction or formal information, we simply designed our own ritual, producing our first rite of passage program in August of 1975 at Northside Baptist Church in Irving, Texas. We named the program "Pai-Charis," a Greek term meaning son of grace.[2] This name stayed with the program for over twenty years.

No one had ever done exactly what Jim and I were doing, exactly the way we were doing it, so who was to tell us that we were doing it wrong? We hammered out the ideas together, sitting on the side of his bed, or hanging our feet over the edge of the swimming pool in our neighborhood complex. When I remember the fun we had, putting symbols and words to the changes taking place inside Jim, I still feel a sense of awe at how we pulled it off. Ten years and a thousand gray hairs later, when Jim was graduating from Officer's Candidate School in the U. S. Navy, the speaker at his commencement ceremony said it best. "If you are not having fun, you are doing it wrong!"[3] We were having fun, so we must have been doing something right. It gave us a sense of achievement to be doing something this important for the first time. We felt like pioneers, and at the same time we felt connected to fathers and sons of ages past.

Our rite of passage program has taken several forms over the twenty-plus years of development, but one thing has not changed. It is the process, not the program that is important. Our original program was built around Jim's relationship with God and with our family. The main emphasis of Jim's rite of passage program was on his personal relationship with God the perfect father, modeled by Jesus Christ, the perfect son. We chose some Bible verses for Jim to memorize, acknowledging God's view of Jim's adult relationships with his family members, the Church, and the world at large.

Jim wrote a short speech, verbalizing the process he was going through. In the speech, he talked about how his relationship with me, his earthly dad, prepared him for his role as an adult male. The speech notified the world that he had been thinking about his entrance into manhood, and that he was ready to make the passage. As part of the preparation, Jim helped me plan a ceremony that would be what a wedding is to a marriage, or what an ordination service is to a ministerial candidate. The ceremony would include singing, testimonies, a message preached by our family pastor, and a public blessing from me, his dad—presenting him to the world as a man. As important as the ceremony is to the rite of passage program, the period of preparation made the program memorable. It gave us a sense of direction as we looked forward to the day of the "Father's Blessing." We even kept a count-down calendar as part of our original workbook.

In the pages that follow, I will give you an in-depth look into that process, which included outings alone as father and son. It included talks, planned and unplanned, about self-image, sexuality, finances, dating, sports, and many other subjects. We talked to a lot of people about what we were doing. Mostly, though, we talked with each other about what it means to be a man. I told Jim about my childhood and many of the difficulties I encountered during my turbulent maturing years. We kept mementos and photos of special times we spent together. We wrote in notebooks about our feelings and our experiences. I told Jim the truth—that I really didn't know how to do this, and that we might be doing it wrong. But many years later, Jim told me that he felt a sense of pride. We were attempting a 'formal' rite of passage program that none of his friends' dads were doing for their sons, and it made him feel special. That's the real core of the ManTracks program, publicizing and formalizing a gut-level respect and love for one another the way God intended it to be. Father and son, facing life together, constructing the most effective discipleship program ever designed, at the workbench of God's first and foremost institution, the home.

I felt special, too. I still do, half a lifetime later. I remember the sheer joy of lying on our backs in sleeping bags and looking up at the Milky Way, listening to the sounds of crickets and frogs griping at one another. Or laughing over the fact that I went to elaborate steps to teach Jim how to fish, but he caught 'em and I didn't.

These private times alone created a perfect environment for discussions on intimate issues.

I was not experienced at this because I did not have a good model to cast this program from. I really didn't know how to do what I was doing. But doing it gave me a confidence I didn't know I had. You have in your hands the benefit of those trial and error times. The questions following each chapter will give you plenty of conversation starters to help you over the humps many fathers and sons find difficult.

Your ManTracks Digest contains guidelines, called Milestones, to help you step-by-step through the simple procedure. The main thing is for you as father and son to concentrate on your relationship for several months. Don't rush the process. You will be two men, shoulder-to-shoulder, working on an important project together. Two men—never forgetting that one is father and one is son—yet working diligently to hammer out a new context for that relationship. As the son becomes more mature, and the dad develops the attitude of a guide, the coming of age process will be an unforgettable experience. ManTracks will include several items that will challenge your time and priority.

You will get mom involved in the process along the way, and you will undoubtedly confront some difficult issues, but you will overcome them together. Through it all you will establish a life-long friendship. You are creating a rite of passage, celebrating a lad's coming of age as a man, but you are also creating a legacy, leaving manhood tracks for the next generation to follow. Oh, and one more thing, dads find this program to be just as much for them as for their sons. There was nothing like this when you were growing up. Don't you wish there had been? Well, now there is. Mantracks cannot make men of boys, but it can give you a track to run on, a path to follow so that your relationship will take on new meaning. The future looks bright. We can have hope that Christianity is being preserved by real men. Godly men who, although not perfect, have a handle on who they are and what they are charged to do with their manhood. It has always been true, and will continue to be so, that young men will rise to the challenge of their generational duty. They will have the courage and maturity to be men of integrity, partly because of the investment their father made in their masculine development. ManTracks can have a lot to do with helping that process along.

Reflections ...

Respond to the questions below by writing in your own notebooks then discuss the ideas you have written when you are alone together.

- What one-on-one times do you enjoy the most as father and son?

- What special incidents in the past year could have been identified as a rite of passage?

- What mementos (pictures, etc.) have you kept from special outings the two of you have experienced together?

CHAPTER 2

The First Mantracks Ceremony

When the day finally came for Jim's rite of passage ceremony, we were all a little nervous. This had never been attempted in our church group, and we were not sure it would be very important to anyone except us. We had planned the ceremony carefully, and sent out formal invitations (like the ones in the Appendix[1]). We sent them to our relatives, Jim's friends at school and his church youth group. My friends at work, and our social friends all got an invitation. Also, we put an invitation in our church bulletin. Still, we were anxious. Would anyone care? I started to worry that no one would come. Jim and I were waiting for the ceremony in a choir room behind the pulpit area in our church, and we could not see the chapel from where we were.

I envisioned a few straggling family members scattered among empty pews. I was afraid the sound system would squeal or the air conditioning would not be on. I think I started to pace the floor. We stood around those last few minutes, kind of like the groom's party at a wedding. Jim started looking over his speech, and I was looking for something to do.

"Everything is going to be just fine, so stop fretting."

I looked around and saw our family pastor coming toward us. His boyish smile gave me reassurance. Rev. Malone was very helpful through the planning and preparation stages, and I knew he would be supportive now. He loved new things, especially things that honored Jesus Christ, and that is exactly what this program was designed to do. His firm grip on my wet palm seemed to calm me down. I had worked hard for this moment, and it was really good to have my pastor believe in me and help me honor my son on this special day.

We went out to take our places in the chapel. My heart leaped for joy. The chapel was full of familiar smiling faces, row after row of them. Friends, family, and church members, all curious and anxiously waiting for the strange ceremony to begin. I breathed a sigh of relief and my mind focused on the "Father's Blessing" that I would deliver in a few minutes.

Because this first program was one we had never seen done before, the youth director Jim chose to be the Master of Ceremonies actually read from a simple explanation I had written for him. It informed the audience of the process that occurred during the previous few months as Jim and I participated in Jim's "Milestones." Later in this book I will discuss all the details of having a good ceremony; one that your son will never forget. Just to satisfy your curiosity, though, I will end this chapter with the blessing I gave Jim at his ceremony. Here is what I said as I stood beside Jim, placed my hands on his shoulders and blessed him publicly:

"Today is a special day. Jim, you are not really grown yet, but you are no longer a boy. By this event, you are being

welcomed into the kingdom of men. The time has come to recognize your adult manhood... So, before God Almighty, maker of heaven and earth, the One who created you man, I pronounce your coming of age as a man. From this time forward, wherever you go, hold your head erect and your shoulders high. You are a man. You have entered the realm of male adults, and you are now responsible to accept as your own the challenge from First Corinthians, chapter sixteen and verse thirteen and fourteen: 'Be on your guard; stand firm in the faith; be [a man] of courage; be strong. Whatever you do, do in love.' Jim, It is my distinct pleasure to pronounce to the world that you are my son in whom I am well pleased. Even as you receive my blessing, I let the world know that now you are a man, my son."

As I was writing this chapter, I asked Jim to write me a letter that I could include in my book to emphasize the spirit of the ManTracks program and ceremony from his point of view. After twenty years, Jim—the first son ever to experience a ManTracks ceremony—might have an insight or two for fathers and sons who are considering a rite-of-passage. He responded to my request, addressing his remarks more to you than me. Here is what he said:

"Dear ManTracks Readers,

My name is James Ray Benton, Jr. I am the first person ever to go through a ManTracks program. My dad, the author of this book designed the program just for me. He asked me to write my thoughts about my ManTracks experience. You have already read that we named my program "Pai-Charis," but the program name is not the important thing. The important thing is the relationship emphasis this kind of ceremony insists that you build as a father and son.

That is what I remember most about my program. There is so much to say, I hardly know where to begin. However, since my remarks must be brief, I want to say something about the guts of a program like this one. Becoming a man is about accepting responsibility, and learning to live within one's own value structure. It is about feeling significant and the need to belong to a family and have the internal resources to be the leader of a new family unit at the same time. Its about being an independent individual, whose parents have granted the blessing of making your own decisions, but always having them there to help if you need input.

My own ManTracks program was much more than I can put into words. It was about the man I call dad (who is in reality my step-dad) and me, working together on a project that I did not understand all the implications of until many years later. As a United States Navy Officer, I have traveled to many foreign countries and interacted with many cultures over the past ten years. In most every one of them I have sensed a spontaneous father-son relationship that just doesn't exist in America in the same sense.

Ellis Hackler did something with me that means more today than it did in 1976. He affirmed me as a male adult when I was just beginning to struggle with the identity thing. I think what that did was cause me to have one less problem to deal with during those crazy years most teens and pre-adults experience. It did not "make me a man," but it did cause me to see myself as fully accepted in the world of men. It gave me a sense of joining the club of older men that every young man feels left out of. I will always be grateful for that feeling.

When I think of my program, I think of that relationship with my dad, who really did "let me go" in the sense that I was trusted. The trust he and my mother placed in me caused me to want to make adult choices and be responsible. I cannot speak for all men, but for me, that is what being a man is all about.

So, you guys get into this program. It is much more elaborate than what I had, but it is basically the same. It gives you a chance to discuss manhood issues and take some clear

steps that will lead to feelings of strength and manly atti-
tudes. It's what you want—the opportunity to be called a
man by the most significant other man in your life, your dad.
Go for it!
  God Bless you,
  Jim."

Reflections ...

Respond to the questions below by writing in your own notebooks then discuss the ideas you have written when you are alone together.

• What thoughts or ideas did Jim's letter bring up for you?

• Where would you conduct your ManTracks cere-mony?

• What items, if any would you include in the passage ceremony that were not mentioned in this overview?

• Who might be included in your ceremony?

• Are there ex-in-laws or step-parents that need to be considered? Before you contact them, read the last chapter of this book. There are some helpful hints there for "blended" family situations.

CHAPTER 3

The Purpose of Milestones

The wind was changing from its gentle westerly direction, alerting the trail guide that he should turn back for camp right away. The riders would protest, but not for long. The rumbling in that dark cloud verified the guide's concern. I knew it meant a *norther* would be blowing in soon. It can happen quickly in the early summer at Horn Creek.[1] We came here every June on a family vacation, and sometimes winter was reluctant to give way to us. Jim, Mark and Ray were about to learn an object lesson about life from this experience. As their dad, I was always looking for object lessons, and this was going to be a duzzie. When Eddie turned his horse off the main trail, every horse in the eight-person party expressed an objection. Horses in a riding stable get in a routine and they don't like for you to change it. When their nose is headed toward the barn, they know they are going home and it takes a fair rider to veto their direction. I was certain Eddie knew what he was doing, but being a dad, I thought I ought to ask him anyway.

"This is a short cut down the mountain," He read my mind before I opened my mouth. "Its not as pretty, but its a lot faster." He twisted his head around to look high above the tall firs, to glance at the boiling clouds, now coming out of the north. "Wind's pickn' up," he mumbled, "We probably ain't gonna' make it before the bottom falls outta' that cloud."

I turned my head to look and felt the clean, crisp air across my face. "Yep." I responded, not knowing very much cowboy-ese. "It looks like we might get a little bit wet. No biggie, we won't melt. This is an adventure, so the boys and me aren't worried." Jim, Mark and Ray were fighting at their various mounts, trying to get them to follow Eddie instead of the familiar trail. I grinned and braced myself for a new adventure.

We slowly twisted across the rock-strewn grass, following our guide for about a mile when the rain started to fall. It came gently at first, then began to gush. "In Texas we'd call this a real *gully-washer*," I shouted through the downpour.

Eddie pulled up and checked his surroundings. He seemed to be looking for something. We had all simply surrendered to the downpour. Every stitch of our clothing was wet through and through, but our spirits were high. This was fun! Unfortunately it wasn't so much fun for the two girls and their mom who made up our riding party, but we 'men' were having a ball.

"Here it is!" he said more to himself than to anyone else. He was pointing a wet finger at a mound of rocks. "That's MileStone number one—We got two more 't go and we'll be home."

"Did some one set the markers so you could use them for a time like this?" I asked over the squeals of the girls and rain splashing on the pile of round smooth rocks. "No," he said. "This is where I buried my pup last spring. She died of the mange."

We rode in silence for a few hundred yards, single file following our guide. The rain let up a bit but continued to come down in a steady, persistent flow, letting us know who was the real boss in these parts. We passed two more mounds of rocks, similar to the first one, just as Eddie said we would. We were back at the barn in short order. The girls headed for the cabins at Mountain Meadow to clean up and find an alternate plan for play. My boys and I stayed for a while in the barn, helping Eddie stow the wet gear, and put the horses back into the corral. My curiosity had the best of me by the time we finished. We sat resting on a bale of hay in the barn, soaking wet but not caring. Jim, Mark, and Ray took off for our cabin, and I asked Eddie the inevitable question. "What is buried in the other two rock piles?" I asked. I was sure there was a life-lesson in this, and I was trying to glean it out.

"I don't rightly know what's in that last 'un," he said, picking at a splinter in his hand with his pocket knife. "The Zeller's have somethin' buried in the middle one, I think." Eddie leaned back on one elbow and began to chew on a straw. "When they first come here in '56, I was their wrangler. We had two ole horses...Them Zellers, they was a green bunch of folks..." he chuckled, reminiscing. "But after that first hard winter, they dug their heels in and learned how to run a Christian camp better 'n anybody I ever saw...Them rock piles must be there so they could remember somethin' they lost here, I reckon, like my little pooch..."

So they could remember. That is exactly what the Old Testament writers recorded as God's command for the Israelites. Some of God's most significant covenant promises were sealed with a monument of rocks. Those rocks became a memory-jogger for the current generation, and a history lesson for future generations. Later that night, I sat with my boys and showed them the connection between the pile of rocks, our guide, and our life. Eddie's pile of rocks were both a memorial and a guide-marker. They helped him remember, and they kept him from getting lost.

The Christian community has a rich heritage in the Old Testament. Although God does not require New Testament saints to live by the Law of Moses, we do have the privilege to adopt some of the pictures and principles from the pre-Christian era. One pictorial principle comes from the story in the third and fourth chapters of the book of Joshua. This Old Testament narrative is a good background model for the principles upon which ManTracks is based.

The people of Israel were about to cross over the Jordan to take possession of the promised land. The Bible says in Joshua 3:14-16:

"So when the people broke camp to cross the Jordan, the priests carrying the ark of the covenant went ahead of them. Now the Jordan is at flood stage all during harvest. Yet as soon as the priests who carried the ark reached the Jordan and their feet touched the water's edge, the water from upstream stopped flowing. It piled up in a heap a great distance away, at a town called Adam in the vicinity of Zarethan, while the water flowing down to the Sea of the Arabah (the Salt Sea) was completely cut off. So the people crossed over opposite Jericho."

Can we fathom such a thing? The water did not just stop flowing. That would be no miracle. Many a river has dried up before and since. No, it was much more than that. The river stopped flowing because it "piled up in a heap." The invisible hand of God just reached out and touched the river and the water stood up like it was behind a Huge transparent dam!

The people of Israel knew that they were a chosen nation. The LORD had visited Moses and sent him to deliver the sons of Jacob from the bondage of the Egyptians. The Israelites had been a slave state for over four-hundred years. After their delivery from Egypt, the Jews witnessed their most dramatic miracle, the crossing of the Red Sea. God dried up the sea, and the entire nation crossed on dry land. Then when the Egyptian army tried to follow, God closed the sea wall, drowning the entire Egyptian army. Now, in the present story, the priests who carried the ark of the covenant of the LORD, standing firm on dry ground in the middle of the Jordan river, had been children who crossed the Red Sea with their parents following behind Moses. God told Joshua,

"Choose twelve men from among the people, one from each tribe, and tell them to take up twelve stones from the middle of the Jordan from right where the priests stood and to carry them over with you and put them down at the place where you stay tonight."

So Joshua called together the twelve men he had appointed from the Israelites, one from each tribe, and said to them,

"Go over before the ark of the LORD your God into the middle of the Jordan. Each of you is to take up a stone on his shoulder, according to the number of the tribes of the Israelites, to serve as a sign among you. In the future, when your children ask you, 'What do these stones mean?' tell them that the flow of the Jordan was cut off before the ark of the covenant of the LORD. When it crossed the Jordan, the waters of the Jordan were cut off. These stones are to be a memorial to the people of Israel forever... So the Israelites did as Joshua commanded them. They took twelve stones

*from the middle of the Jordan, according to the number of
the tribes of the Israelites, as the LORD had told Joshua;
and they carried them over with them to their camp,
where they put them down. Joshua set up the twelve stones
that had been in the middle of the Jordan at the spot where
the priests who carried the ark of the covenant had stood.
And they are there to this day."*

This story provides an excellent visual for the
ManTracks program. The stones in the story had no
meaning beyond their symbolic reference to a great
miracle of God. The purpose of the stones is obvious
from the text. They were a memorial. The Israelites did
not have access to a 35mm camera. There was no way
every father in all of Israel could "capture" the memory
and hand it forward to his sons and daughters in a tan-
gible way. The verbal procedure God designed was
anchored to the rocks that were set up for a memorial.
It was a ritual, plain and simple. The son was to ask the
father,

"Hey, dad, what's the meaning of this pile of rocks?"
(He was taught to say that from earliest memory.)

Dad responds, "I'm glad you asked, son. Those are
memory rocks." Then he proceeded to tell the entire
story, whether the son really wanted to hear it or not.
It was their way of preserving a memory.

We need memorials. They help us set boundaries
and guide us in our daily lives. Family picture albums
are godly stuff. They are ways to go back in time and
re-live the important moments. Like our family times
in Horn Creek. In seven or eight years, we established
a memory as sure as the pile of rocks by the Jordan in
Israel. The pictures in our album of our times at Horn
Creek has provided memory-joggers to remind us of
those good times when our family bonded and grew.

This is what The ManTracks Digest is all about. It is a memory-keeper. Both fathers and sons will set some very important 'stones' during this process, things they will remember the rest of their lives. And the memory will live on. A fair-haired little girl or a shaggy-headed little boy will snuggle up next to a loving grandpa on some couch in a living room a generation from now. Little fingers will point at some funny picture, and proud old eyes will mist with memory.

"That's your dad and me when I was going through a 'rite of passage' program with your daddy. Some day, your daddy will do this for you..."

We remember bits of time, seconds really. Our brains are not equipped to handle large volumes of detail about some isolated incident that happened fifty years ago. But we do remember moments with the aid of a good memory-jogger. Today's memorials are glossy colored images tucked away in padded family albums. If we lived in eighth century Israel it would have been a pile of rocks in a certain location. The meaning is the same; it is so we can remember.

Your ManTracks Digest is such a tool. Each completed lesson is like a pile of stones that reminds us of where we have been. It is a memorial. The father-son projects are called Milestones because they provide a visual aid, a memory jogger for your progress. Each time you complete one of the Milestones toward your coming of age ceremony, you do much more than check it off in the ManTracks Digest. You add a stone to your memorial. A memory. Isolated, unorganized, these individual events get lost in the flurry of life in the fast lane, but together, these memorials provide proof that you have stepped through some hoops, made some preparations, had a ceremony. As the son in the program, you might not be too impressed with the whole thing right now, but later on, when time sneaks up on you and whispers some question in your ear about your manhood, you will answer with the memory of dad's hand on your shoulder, blessing you and announcing your arrival into the kingdom of men.

There are dozens of things this program could have included. Some people will look it over and say its too naive. Some will criticize it because it is too focused on the spiritual, some will say it is not spiritual enough. Critics have asked why there is not more in the program about psychological development. On and on it goes. But my humble response is to point two directions. First I point backwards. In 1976, when my first son was experiencing the puzzling pains of puberty, I was determined to help him take charge of his manhood. I refused to stand idly by and just hope he navigated the passage, becoming a real man in a world of emasculates, a godly man in a world of spiritual wimps. He needed help, like every boy in the world. The help might not necessarily be in the form of a specific program like ManTracks, but it did include positive male images he could identify with. We did this thing, and it was good enough! Then I point forward.

The future of manhood is frighteningly questionable. I'm not talking about the physical. There will always be a "Y" chromosome to contribute to half of the genetic make-up of the little tike that wriggles out of the womb. I am referring to the almost lost art of malehood. Every thinking man is concerned about it. Religious and secular leaders, alike speak in the same way to this fear. Robert Bly, one of the foremost spokesmen for the New Age men's movement, said,

"...it is clear to men that the images of adult manhood given by the popular culture are worn out; a man can no longer depend on them. By the time a man is thirty-five he knows that the images of the right man, the tough man, the true man which he received in high school do not work in life. Such a man is open to new visions of what a man is or could be."[2]

Even though I do not agree with much of the data that comes in the form of authoritative print from men who do not put Jesus Christ in their paradigm, I do agree with this statement as far as it goes. I must say, however, I am appalled at the way many authors of the secular men's movement have approached the kingdom of men. The movement seems to be a knee-jerk- reaction to the feminist movement, which began in the early sixty's and had its strongest hey-day when my sons were navigating their way through puberty. Like most men of twenty years ago, I felt attacked and put down because I was a man. Many men tell me they experienced the same thing. It was as though we needed to apologize for being male! Something had to be done, not something political, something Spiritual. If Jimmy, Mark, and Raymond (my boys) were going to cast off the 'old images' (as Robert Bly puts it) of manhood, what would they replace it with? Look at the answer for most young men of that day. Many have lost more than their youth since 1976. It would be boring to quote the statistics you already know. The divorce rate for instance, not only points to a softening of the American public's attitude about marriage laws. It also points to boys who grew into adult males, but never assumed their responsible role as man. While I am on my soap box, I may as well say it like it really is. If Christians want to significantly lower the divorce rate, practically end father-abandonment and reduce single-parent homes, then let us began a wholesale crusade to train the young men of our nation to be responsible adult males. That is how ManTracks can be a truly helpful program in Christian homes, churches and communities.

Men need tools to do the work of fatherhood. In the gray light of perception when we realize we are both our father's son and our son's father, there is a moment of panic. Men quietly admit to themselves that they do not know how to be a man. Passing manhood on to this precious bundle of life is more frightening than just walking manhood alone.

We are molding men. We simply cannot ignore the Creator's design in search of a better mold. The 'sixties and 'seventies tried to hand men a Godless blue-print. But when we unrolled it on the work-bench of our own home, it was blank. The instructions said 'create your own.' Today, that blueprint has been tossed aside. Many dads have gone back to Proverbs and Timothy. Our sons have not all walked exactly as we would have liked over the past few years, but the mold in which their manhood was cast is true. The Holy Spirit of Almighty God has His blueprint stamp on each of their hearts, and they are more than adult males. They are men! Like your sons, they are not products of a program. They are property of the King of Kings and Lord of Lords. However, the program was a guide. I used it to keep myself anchored to the Lord's paradigm. I do not take up an argument against my critics, but until they come up with a better program, I will promote this one.

Work through the program page by page. You will reap optimum benefit by staying on schedule. The instructions are intended to take some time. The ManTracks Milestones are challenging, but well worth the effort.

Each Milestone contains guidelines for relational activity and spiritual growth.

The Spiritual question in each Milestone has a Bible-related project to complete. Some require father and son to work together, some are designed for solo. The son in the ManTracks program will be challenged to understand, and be able to verbalize his adult masculine relationship with God the perfect Father, Jesus, the perfect Son, and God the Holy Spirit, representing the perfect family. Together, you will examine his identification with the Body of Christ, and outline the events surrounding his Spiritual birth. He will be required to discuss the relationship adult men have with all the various other members of the Body of Christ.

Each Milestone will challenge the son to look inside himself, working on feelings, self-esteem issues, and family relationships. Father acts as the guide through this program. Together, you will complete an informal study of what being a man means in terms of emotions and feelings. You will find challenging communication exercises in this section.

When you have completed your twelve Milestones you will have a record of the memories the two of you have developed. The finished product will contain pictures, memoirs, souvenirs, artwork or a combination of things you want in it. Journalizing is the one constant for all twelve milestones. You each have your own notebook to record your answers to the Milestone questions. You will compare and discuss them when you meet together in your relational time. At the end, you will write a combination of your ideas in your ManTracks Digest.

A word to dads...

Certainly you cannot wait for someone else to guide your son through his manhood passage. They (whomever they are) will botch it. Every son was born into this world with a father need. You were, and so was your son. Only dad can do the best job in filling that need. God is so gracious that He does in many cases provide a surrogate-dad, a-foster dad, or (as in my son's case), a step-dad. The reality is there are no perfect dads. Your responsibility began before your son (or step-son) came into this world, or under your influence, and God in His infinite wisdom has provided you with all the equipment you need to guide that lad to full adulthood. You can do it. For your son's sake, you must do it. Stu Weber, who has encouraged men everywhere with his best seller, *Tender Warrior*, said in his latest book, *Locking Arms,*

"Real men leave clear tracks—big, steady tracks—that others can follow... Different men leave different tracks. Some of us tend to walk so lightly—like Tolkein's light-footed elves—we leave little or no impression at all. Others walk so erratically there's no clear path for anyone to follow. Others walk so heavily they crush all around them. Like driverless bulldozers locked in gear, they leave a path of random destruction in their wake..."[3]

Stu, as usual you're right on. Real men do leave tracks. Some godly men leave ManTracks.

Reflections ...

Respond to the questions below by writing in your own notebooks then discuss the ideas you have written when you are alone together.

- How does the story about the short-cut down the mountain trail relate to the Bible story about the miracle of the memorial stones at the river Jordan? What do the two stories have in common?

- What kind of memory-jogger would Jim (age 12), Mark (age 8), and Ray (age 7) need to remind them of what they experienced on that mountain trail, almost twenty years ago?

- How will having a ManTrack Digest help you preserve important events in your father-son relationship?

- Why, would you go to all the trouble to go through a course like ManTracks?

CHAPTER 4

Rituals and Family Albums

A Family Tradition Is Born

Jim's program was a success. He started acting more like a man and our family began to treat him more like a man. Other people became interested in our rite of passage program for bringing young men into manhood, and we helped several other father and son teams. Four years passed before we began a rite of passage program with our second son Mark. Donald Mark Neace was also my stepson, but like Jim I could never consider him any different than a biological family member.

If you have more than one child you will agree with me that they are always different. The second is never like the first, and Mark was certainly unique. He naturally wanted the same attention given him as he witnessed his big brother getting four years earlier, but he wanted a slightly different program. We had the benefit of Jim's ritual to work from, so Mark's was a little easier than if we had started from scratch. We set up some check points to help us follow the procedure we had created for Jim's program, and these became the nucleus of what is now the Milestone program.

I asked Mark to give his point of view about his own rite of passage program, and he wrote the following letter:
"To ManTracks Readers:

Hello. My name is Donald Mark Neace. My dad died in an airplane crash when I was two years old. I don't remember him, but I am sure he was a good man because he married my mom, and they had me! So when mother married Ellis Hackler I was four years old. That is why Ellis is the person I call dad. He has always been my friend. I am closer to him now than at anytime in my life.

At 27, I have not always lived the way he raised me (although I never went very far!), but he has always loved me no matter where I went or what I did. I will always be grateful for that. In 1993, Dad and I were at the Promise Keepers® conference in Boulder, Colorado. It was a spectacular event; but what I remember most about that great conference of fifty-thousand men lifting their voices and singing to God, was not the stadium event, it was the event that occurred in a tiny college dorm room we were sharing that weekend. Dad and I were alone in that room, just talking about life and the past. I remember telling him what I now tell the world: I will always be grateful for my coming-of-age program dad led me through. It has been an anchor to hold me to the truth of God's word and to my family over the years.

I remember the times at Horn Creek, where we as a family spent one week out of every summer when I was growing up. Dad may not have intended, or realized it then, but those were family rituals that will always stick with me.

I may never be the "evangelist-type" (that dad probably secretly hoped I'd be) but I am something better. I am me. A me whom Dad loves and accepts just as I am. As a man, I never question my masculine image because of my strong relationship with dad.

I recommend that you fathers and sons take advantage of this program. The best thing it will do for you is get you together and cause you to talk about life together. Young men will grow to be adult men who believe in themselves, trust God and dare to dream big dreams and accomplish great things, because they have a solid relationship with their dad. They can explore their world because dad has set them free to be themselves, yet, he is never far away to lend wisdom when asked and strength when needed.—Oh, by the way— my dad and I sat in the pouring rain at Candlestick Park and saw the last game Joe Montana played in a 'Niner uniform. 'Talk about memorable events! That ranks up there with all the mountain top experiences we ever had. I'll tell you something else. We are not through. The future events we will do together will be filled with just as much joy as the past, because we have a relationship any father and son would be proud of. Right dad?

God Bless You.

Mark. "

The idea of organizing the discussion questions and relational interaction into "Milestones" came along later. In fact it came up through a Bible study Deanna and I were in several years after Mark's program. Deanna gets the credit for first making the connection of the Israelites crossing Jordan and placing memorial stones at the crossing, to modern memory joggers for our rite of passage program. As our son's mom she had participated intimately in each program (in fact, she is responsible for the idea of mothers and sons going on a date as one of the milestones).

Moms provide the feminine view, and their input is invaluable. Her support is so necessary that the program should be aborted and placed on hold if mom does not wish to participate, or cannot give her support. The father and step-son situation requires special emphasis. We will cover this model in more detail in Chapter 23.

When our number three son, Raymond,[1] two years later begin to work on his ManTracks program, (it was still called Pai-Charis), we had the rite of passage steps designed rather well. Some things were modified each time, we worked with fathers and sons on their programs, and others ideas were added or deleted along the way. Mostly, however, various Milestones only needed duplicated and personalized to make the program work well for the third and final ManTracks program for our family. The invitation cards, for instance, were redesigned. Also the location and participants changed (we included Raymond's birth-mother and his step-father in the ceremony), but no major program changes were made. The process was more fun because we were spending more time together, rather than working on the details of the program design. Plus, I had the wisdom of the other two "vets," Raymond's brothers, who had already completed their programs. Here is what Raymond has to say about his ManTracks program:

From: *Raymond Ellis Hackler, Cpt., U.S. Army*
To: *Fathers and sons interested in the*
                ManTracks Program
Subj: *A letter to be used in the ManTracks book.*
                My view of the Rite of Passage Program By
                Raymond Hackler

"Being a man is about choosing responsibility. As a boy grows into a man, he finds greater levels of responsibility waiting at every stage of the development. It waits for him at

school, in the workplace, in the home, and in his personal and spiritual life. The wise man - indeed, the real man -is the one who freely accepts these responsibilities. He is easily recognized in the misguided, immoral crowd of today: the disciplined student; the reliable and honest employee; the faithful, loving husband and father; the dedicated Christian.

The ManTracks (formerly "Pai- Charis") ceremony is one way to indoctrinate a boy into this new world of compounded responsibility. Similar in concept to the Jewish Bar Mitzvah, ManTracks is essentially a ceremony honoring the passage of a Christian boy into Christian manhood.

As for as I know, my dad is the only man I ever knew of who had this ceremony for his sons. He designed it to be strategically placed early in a boy's developing-manhood years, after the start of adolescence, but before the boy reaches the age where he can work or date. In this way the boy, already aware of the physical changes taking place in his body, is further enlightened to the upcoming challenges he will face in the years to come.

I went through this ceremony when I was fourteen years old, as did my two older step-brothers. Their perspective may vary slightly from mine, but to me the message was clear: seek out wisdom and responsibility. There have never been more significant words for me than when my dad placed his hands on my shoulders and blessed me before the world. I will never forget his words, 'and now you are a man, my son.'

Of course I had more growing to do, I still am growing, even after the demanding position I hold as an officer in the U.S. Army; but the ambiguity of knowing my masculine character, as I have witnessed in other men, is settled. I am a man, I have passed through a rite of passage my dad designed for me. I look back on it as a memorial of great significance and I continue to draw strength from it.

51

There is one other important and lasting impression I took from my rite of passage program. As I gave my short speech during the ceremony, I looked out and saw dozens of loving faces. These were my immediate and extended family, close family friends, and church friends, and they were all there because they cared about me. I realized then that I could, and should, rely on these people to help me through the rough years ahead. Many of them did just that. I am who I am today because of God's love, their love, and parents who cared enough to prepare me for the future.

God Bless You All,
Raymond"

As you can see, although it has been many years since their ceremony, all three of my sons testify that the ManTracks program made a dramatic and significant impact on their lives. They agree that the memory of that special day continues to give them a balanced sense of belonging and self-reliance. Being a man is not easy, but my sons tell me that because they had a program like ManTracks to mark their manhood passage, they never question their masculine adulthood.

ManTracks will help rectify the dilemma you face, just as those original programs helped my sons gain a perspective of their manhood. The instructions in ManTracks will help fathers and sons work together on a unique "Becoming a man of God" program. It is flexible enough for you to deviate from the program and go your own way if you choose. Or you can stick with every line, and complete each question. The benefits of the ManTracks program are self evident.

The major purpose of The ManTracks Digest is to set the stage for the ManTracks Ceremony. This is the climax of several months of concentrated energy, focused on a relationship that is far too rare in our society—sons and fathers spending the kind of time in one short period that is reminiscent of pre-industrial revolution days, when dad earned a living close to the home, and children could be near him most of the day. Many evenings were spent together, laughing, reading, talking and playing, not watching TV, or isolated behind earphones. Sons developed a healthy understanding of their sexuality by observing the warm looks and gentle touches between mom and dad, as natural as rain, and as fulfilling as heaven.

The ceremony will celebrate the end of that special time when dad and son took great effort to be together. They will commemorate special family traditions, spontaneously begun and tenaciously hung on to. Like other memories, the ceremony will be rather short, compared to a life-time, but it will last for generations. It will register a point in time when the boy becomes a man.

Naturally, the process of growing from childhood to adulthood is much more than a program that culminates in a ceremony—everyone knows that. In fact one of the most important points we drive home in the ManTracks program is to show the lad that growing into adulthood is a long, slow, and sometimes painful process. He will not really be "adult" when he finishes the program. He will be acknowledged as a MAN versus being a kid, or child, or boy. He will learn that manhood is not counted in years, but in positive experiences that build a bridge between adolescence and adulthood, one plank at a time. The expanse is immense and the dangers are great, but true men of God have paved the way before us with their testimonies of God's love and grace.

With your interactive efforts, working together in the ManTracks program, fathers and sons will have tracks to follow that point men toward adulthood. It will give the son a head start at the next chapter of his life. Because of your spiritual birth, and your sonship in the family of God, you are and always will be a man-child in the school of grace. This book cannot add to that. However, because of the great emphasis God places on relationships[2], the adult male is required to lead out in building relationships, not hang back, as we have seen men do in this century. It will encourage you to strengthen your relationship as father and son.

I urge you to work on The ManTracks Digest as a father-son team. Face the hard issues together. Accept the challenges, keep the appointments with each other, and do the journalizing assignments. Like anything else, you will get from this process what you invest into it. However, unlike any other process we know, ManTracks will provide a pattern for you to follow that will result in an unprecedented bonding experience.

Let the Holy Spirit do His work in and through both of you. After your hard work, this program will greatly reward you, giving dad the formal opportunity to say publicly what every lad desires to hear: "…And now you are a man, my son."

Reflections …

This is a good time to assess your attitude about the ManTracks program so far. Respond to the questions below by writing in your own notebooks then discuss the ideas you have written when you are alone together.

- How do you feel about the several month commitment required to do the ManTracks program?

- Do you think you are ready to go forward with this program? Please state why or why not.

- What other things compete for your time; things that might interfere with the progress of ManTracks?

- What long-term value do these competing things hold?

- What will be done about the lack of time available for a program like this?

CHAPTER 5

Desperately Seeking Dad

We were early and there were plenty of empty seats. The organ was playing a familiar hymn as people were arriving and making internal preparations to worship. I found a good spot and paused while Deanna stepped past me and slid gently into the pew. I had no longer begun to relax in the ray of the sunlit, stained glass window when I heard the commotion behind me. A little boy was objecting to the location his mother had chosen for him to sit.

"Mommie, I can't see through that man!" he protested loudly. He was referring to me, of course and the whole congregation knew it now. His mom finally won the battle, convincing him that if he stood in the pew, and moved slightly to the right he could see over my shoulder. Even so, I could not get that phrase out of my head.

I-can't-see-through-that-man, I thought. An idea was germinating and I must admit, I wrote it down on the white space of the worship bulletin. It's OK, people around me thought I was taking sermon notes. In fact, every so often I would sort of nod my head as I looked at the preacher and back at my notes. What I scratched on that bulletin formed the basis of this chapter. I wonder how well my sons were able to see through me to Jesus Christ. I determined to ask them the next chance I got.

I learned in my study of the human psyche that little children look to dad as if he is God. When a lad is five, dad can do anything. Dad's love that age! It is undoubtedly the best of all periods of time. Our kids actually admire us. We think they are much smarter than their mothers or their grandparents!

John was relaxing in the family room one evening, with his wife and her mother. Timmy, John's eight-year-old, Mr. Know-it-all, abruptly interrupted the conversation by asking John a geography question he couldn't remember the answer to. It has happened to you, and if it hasn't, it will. It never happens when you are alone. Oh no, it is when you are in front of your mother-in-law. Timmy stood across the room and half shouted, "Hey, dad. Where is Gibraltar?" John's reign as superdad had been slipping gradually over the past couple of years, and now he was about to be officially dethroned.

All eyes turn to John. Mom's, baby sister's, mother-in-law's, God's…

"Uh, well, uh. Lets see. Uh, I think its, umm, nope. Its…" (Its too late! Sister giggled, and everybody got a good laugh at dad's expense). John had been upstaged by his own son. His wife, or maybe it was his mother-in-law, made some remark that, although intended as jest, shut John down. He got his male ego bruised. No one knew what being embarrassed in public meant to John. The memory of his alcoholic father, putting him down was too much. He clinched his jaw and quietly walked to the garage. The window that was John, through which Timmy viewed the world had just drawn the shade

Kids can see through you. They see the world through your eyes. They have a view of the vast universe through your transparency. But, if that window closes because dad is absent, emotionally or physically, or because he has been embarrassed, you loose your superman status. I have taken a survey and dad's agree: kids start to loose their wisdom at about age ten or eleven and they don't regain it until they have a child of their own who can ask them an off-the-wall question, catching them off guard.

By the time a dad has been put down a few times, depending on his relationship with his own dad, deep wounds of self-esteem start to become too painful. Dad can't risk being upstaged by his own kid, so he clams up. The transparency window is closed. The child can no longer see through him to the world outside. If that window stays closed, dad gets put aside and Lad starts to seek a window to the world somewhere else. Guess where he goes. You got it, to his friends. His peers whose dads have also recently become stupid.

At first glance, this sounds humorous, but look again. This is where America sets herself apart as a nation. The independent youth culture, rebellious, angry (at dad) and hungry for affection and acceptance, band together to make new heroes out of shirtless, long-haired, dirty, drug-logged rock stars. Because that is the farthest they can get from hard-working, stone-hearted dad, who has gone to the garage to ease his own pain, to experience his own kind of rebellion.

Many men and women go through life emotionally looking for their missing father, desperately seeking dad! Even if dad is at home, he often is not emotionally involved. Men, in general have not really been a part of the child-rearing home life since the industrial revolution. They march off to work as they have marched off to war, and come home tired and beaten.

Budding young men, needing the dad God intended, tromp around the house looking for a father's blessing like searching for a lost toy. Dad is nearby, but oblivious. The hole in his heart is just as big as the one his son is beginning to experience. He never got a blessing from his dad, so he has none to give. He knows something is missing, but he doesn't know what it is. He reaches for his hip pocket and offers what society has demanded that he master in. But material things, without father's blessing, without his love, without the transparency that every child (boy or girl) desperately needs, are ungratefully consumed. The dad window is closed. But work-robot dad continues to provide more of what the child needs least. All through the children's growing years, they have been prevented from seeing life through the man God intended. They go out looking for love in all the wrong places.

Open my counseling file drawer and listen to what some clients have said:

(Bill, age 34) "It is not that he wasn't there. He came home almost every night to the same easy chair. He said he deserved some peace and quiet because he had worked so hard all day. I often wanted to sit with him, but I never felt wanted. My dad didn't run around on my mom—he just had a love affair with the TV set."

(Aaron, age 40) "Dad was a long-haul trucker. People who knew him said he could turn a truck on a dime and give you change back. He bragged about being able to stay awake longer than any other driver, getting that extra mile. But to me, he was simply missing in action. He never once saw me play ball. Never came to a school play. Its strange… I have

said for years that I would never be like my dad; but I find myself wrapped up in my work and avoiding the things my kids need me the most for, emotional connection. I guess I have turned out to be just like dad..."

(Millie, age 44) "After everyone had gone home following my 40th birthday party, and I was alone with my thoughts, I wondered when I would finally grow away from my longing to have my dad at these special events. You know, he never came to them...I think it embarrassed him to be around a lot of people. But I interpreted it to mean that he didn't love me. Why do men grow up like that? I see the same kind of thing in my husband and also in his dad. What is it with men?"[1]

Good question, what is it with men? Society is sending some confusing messages to men today. Who wouldn't be confused? The rules may not be nailed to the Post Office door, but all men know the Ten Commandments of the American man:

1. Thou shalt not cry, for tears are an abomination in the sight of Mascule, thy god.

2. Thou shalt not display weakness, for weakness is the characteristic of Femina, thy enemy.

3. Thou shalt not need affection, neither gentleness nor warmth, for thou art self-sufficient.

4. Thou shalt be needed by others, but thou shall need no other person, neither woman, nor man.

5. Thou shalt comfort thy wife and thy children, even thy neighbor's children, but thou shalt need no comfort.

6. Thou shall be steel, not flesh.

7. Thou shall be perfect in thy manhood, remember thy maleness and be driven by it always.

8. Thou shall stand alone.

9. Be thou competitive in all things. Play to win, for there is no second place seats in Mascule's kingdom.

10. Anger shall be thine only emotion, and thou shalt display it often.[2]

Some men think they must display a tough-guy attitude in order to be the leader in their marriage and family. Many men paint themselves into a corner, surrounded on all sides by impossible ideals and unreal expectations. No man could survive for long under this identity.

What is it with men? The cruel god, Mascule has devoured their hearts, and redefined their roles. Femina, their all powerful arch-enemy demands tenderness, feelings-talk, and long hours 'relating' in shopping malls. What is it with men? They go looking for meaning and purpose in the form of a pay-check at work, where they hope to join other men in their search for a father-image, male icon. Someone to show them how to survive. But there, too, more often these days, they run into Femina, and are lied to by Mascule. What is it with men, Indeed!

Men are human beings, seeking relief from guilt, seeking praise for a job well done, seeking affirmation that they are O.K., seeking approval as an individual. Who is to provide these elements? Dad should! Every man and every woman knows intrinsically that dad is the source for competence, self-reliance and inner strength. When he is not present, they have to find these characteristics elsewhere. While mom gives kindness and love; dad provides approval. Mom bequeaths a hospitable spirit, dad trains us to face the elements, unafraid.

Twenty years of counseling people from broken homes has taught me that when a man or a woman lacks competence in the workplace, they very likely had a father who was emotionally absent. If a woman grows up with a fear of men, or an unhealthy disregard for the opposite sex, nine times out of ten, her dad was not there for her. When a man is lost in his work and has little or no emotional connection with his family, avoids intimacy, and has trouble communicating beyond the vernacular of his business, he very often is the adult child of an absent father. These are not random statements. They are supported by a 1994 survey conducted by the National Center for Fathering. Look at just a few of the alarming facts of that survey:

Tonight, almost 40 percent of America's children will go to sleep in the house where their biological father does not live. According to data collected by the National Center for Health Statistics, approximately 29 percent of white and 66 percent of black children are not living with their biological father. More than one-half of all children who do not live with their father have never been in their father's home[3]

These and similar data are embarrassingly abundant. According to the Bureau of Vital Statistics, more than half of all marriages end in divorce, and approximately one-million children will experience their parent's divorce this year. You probably already know that these data are similar in the Christian community.[4] Ask any competent psychologist or Bible-believing sociologist, they will tell you, we are a nation of people desperately seeking dad. In his book, *Man Enough*, Frank Pittman agrees:

Life for most boys and for many grown men is a frustrating search for the lost father who has not yet offered protection, provision, nurturing, modeling, or especially, anointment. All those tough guys who want to scare the world into seeing them as men, and who fill up the jails; all those men who aren't home at home, who don't know how to be a man with a woman, only a brute or a boy, and who fill up the divorce courts; all those corporate raiders and rain-forest burners and war starters who want more in hopes that more will make them feel better... [they] Go through their puberty rituals day after day for a lifetime, waiting for a father to anoint them and say "attaboy," to treat them as good enough to be considered a man.[5]

You may have guessed my thesis by now. We need to establish a new generation of God-fearing dads. Certainly I don't believe ManTracks will work a national miracle. I am not of the illusion that a rite of passage program will solve America's ills, but I do believe we can positively affect the next generation by helping one father at a time establish godly tracks for his son to follow into manhood.

Right now, we are in a heap of trouble, I think you will agree. We are a nation of coachless players blasting into the twenty-first century at warp speed, with no game plan. Not one man in my generation stepped up to the plate with a written model to assist Christian adolescent males with their neophyte manhood.

I invested hundreds of hours in research, looking for the evidence that godly men were focusing on a specific program that would help young men find their masculinity. I found nothing. Of course there were many great books by Christian authors (even more now), some about a man's personal relationship with God, some about a man's relationship with his wife, some about how to share your faith. You will find many of the titles that helped me in my bibliography, but there was nothing like what you now hold in your hand. Nothing.

Don't get me wrong, I am not tooting my own horn or seeking glory. I am blowing a trumpet, calling for godly dads to come out of the woodwork and take a stand. This might not be the best rite of passage program, but I think it beats the humanistic, new age stuff, of the secular men's movement. I have read of men going in bands to the woods and beating tom-toms, smoking something to help them forget how stupid this is, and crying out to the cloud gods. That is why I think a rite of passage program, pointing men to Jesus Christ, uniting fathers and sons in a common cause, and offering specific steps of action that lead to a positive blessing, is so necessary.

This is more than a book, as you already know. It is a program guide to assist you with a rite of passage into adulthood. If you are the son in the program, the questions and projects are designed to help you focus on the responsibilities of adult men in the Body of Christ. When you complete the program, you will have the confidence that you are progressing into adulthood with a purpose. If you are the dad in the program, it will give you step-by-step help to guide your son into and through this important passage. You will have to admit to your son that you never had a program like this, but you are confident that you can be his guide because that is the role God created for you. Together, you will have come to the end of your dad search. Your peers may still be desperately seeking dad, but you are following ManTracks into adulthood. You can stand before the world and say "God is my father, the Church is my family, I am living for Christ, becoming the man God called me to be."

Reflections ...

Respond to the questions below by writing in your own notebooks then discuss the ideas you have written when you are alone together.

Dad:

- In what way or ways are you still desperately seeking your own dad?

- What can you share with your son that will help him understand some of your emotional needs?

- Make the connection between the need for "dad" and the ManTracks program.

Son:

- How do you think a program like ManTracks can help you become a man?

- What do you think a program like this will do for your relationship with your dad?

- Why, in your opinion is a relationship with dad so important in becoming a godly man?

- What expectations do you have about this program, and enhancing your relationship with your dad?

CHAPTER 6

Catching Manhood

"Dad did not teach me how to catch." The young man said with strained voice. "We just never connected—he was always too busy with making a living, that he never took the time to teach me how to live." The young executive had a business degree from a major university and he had a management position in one of the largest computer companies in our area. Still, he was miserable. His nine year-old boy was acting out, crying for dad's attention, home life was in shambles as his second marriage was breaking up. As he slumped deeper into his chair in my office, I listened with love and realized that his dad had indeed shown him how to live. He had shown him the wrong things, but he had thrown life at my friend who caught on very well.

Throwing and catching a baseball might be one of American man's most sacred symbols, because it illustrates so many things about life-training. It has been said that "more is caught than taught" in the process of learning to live. Catching is the ability to handle the various roles of manhood. Through various rituals, a lad learns to be a man. He *catches on* by watching and interacting with older men. By *throwing*, a father trains the son how to *catch*. This analogy brings up a mired of images for all of us. Let's pitch this idea around a bit.

When you were a little tike, your dad would throw the ball a lot differently than when you were trying out for shortstop. The ball tossed lightly gave you, the toddler a feel for catching. It embedded deeply the idea that catching was a big-time responsibility. Woe be to those who didn't learn to catch early on. We missed some of life's most important moments—some learning opportunities that could never be repeated.

Blessed be the dad who praised his little boy for every juvenile attempt at catching. It built self-confidence that the lad would use later to snag a burning fast-ball out of the sky as it blazed from the bat of a would-be homer. On the other hand, fear strikes at the heart of every sand-lot right fielder! Why do you think he is out there instead of crouched low at shortstop? Obviously talent and hustle have something to do with it, but mostly, the little guy is wearing a sign on his ball cap that reads "I have no confidence that I can actually catch a ball. I want to play, but I don't catch very well." OK so they put you in right field. And that's just fine with you because when you were little, dad was gone a lot, and no one was around to teach you how to catch. You never learned how to handle the ball.[1]

What is the ball a symbol of? Life itself. Its being a man in a man's world. We could call it *emotional coordination*. It is the routine responsibilities of every man's day. It is handling finances responsibly, facing competition squarely and honestly; it is dealing with everyday situations with integrity, it is the ability to go one-one-one with the devil in all the temptations of life and be a winner. Its the ability to handle sexual temptation, and the self-empowerment to understand one's own sexuality.

Gosh!, how we right-fielders hated the idea of having the ball come our way. The whole world is watching. God and all the great cloud of witnesses are looking on when the need to be honest, pure, self-confident and self-reliant comes sailing into our turf. Its the right fielder's nightmare. A big-league question comes to mind: how are you going to handle this fly ball. Muff it, and it could cost you your career, your family, your self-esteem. All you have to do is catch it. The problem is there's sun in your eyes and a hole in your glove!

Catching On To Life Responsibilities

There are at least four kinds of *balls* that come flying into right field that every little-leaguer must learn to catch, or field properly before he can play in the big-leagues. They are symbolic of the male-mystique characteristics of

- **provision,**
- **protection**
- **leadership,** and
- **nurturing.**

Each of these represent a different kind of ball coming at every lad. For instance, the characteristic of provision could be represented by the pop fly. It is fairly easy to catch. The player has plenty of time to judge the arc and get his glove in place. This kind of ball is caught from the earliest time in his catching career. Lad sees dad leave the house and stay gone for long hours, then return. He has been at work. Usually this is a ball we men learned to catch before we know what the game is all about. We put provision up there really high in the kingdom of male-dom. In fact, it is so high that it rivals all other male score cards. Men are conditioned to measure their self-worth by the size of their pay-check. There are thousands of symbols of this manhood trap. Cars, houses, club memberships, and name plaques. We pretend that the point is to provide for our family, but we fool no one. The game goes on, and the *provision* pop-fly is the most common kind of ball we have to catch. Many men wind up pitching this ball to themselves. They can be seen out in right field, eye on the wrong ball, and while they are tossing and catching it, the real game goes on—but they don't know what inning it is.

The male characteristic of *protection* could be represented by the smooth grounder. This is perhaps the very easiest ball to field. Protection is a male thing. We are all ready to get our stick and go check on the sounds that go bump in the night and everyone knows that killing spiders is coded in the male genetic DNA. In fact, one of the growth traits that men hold dear is that time in life when we are no longer afraid of the dark. Many people believe that part of becoming a man is sleeping without a night-light! So protection is a rather easy ball to catch, our dads probably did a pretty good job of tossing this one to us. Most men have caught on well.

The male characteristic of *leadership* could be illustrated by the blazing direct hit. This a different kind of ball than providing and protecting. This is a right-fielder's nightmare. The blazing direct hit zooms past the infield at speeds over 90 mph—it's about face-high and you either try to catch it or duck! The right-fielder has to be especially alert to catch it. If he does, he is only doing his job. If he misses, it will continue all the way to the right-field fence, for a ground-rule double. How embarrassing!

The idea of being the leader of the family does not mean being a dictator, being mean, or being dogmatic. It does mean looking further down the road to see where a particular decision will end up. What will be the consequences on me and my family if I make this decision or that. It is a characteristic that has the courage to say, "This way." Often the concept of leadership is very unclear. It is sometimes mistaken for a character trait that requires a certain kind of personality. That is not true. Every man was called by God, and empowered to be a leader. It is a take-charge kind of attitude that requires love and sensitivity toward others, combined with the need to be tough.

Of course, most right fielders have a pretty hard time with this ball. We see most of them chasing it, and chasing it, and chasing it.

Finally, we have the characteristic of *nurturing*. Now this is the very worst kind of ball for our right-fielder to try to handle. It is represented by the crazy hopping grounder. Just about the time you think you have it in your glove, zoom, it bounces up over your head, or to the right or left. The crazy hopping grounder—like nurturing is really tough for a man to learn to handle. Most dads, it seems, just ignored this lesson all together. Nurturing seems feminine.

It takes a special kind of dad to be both nurturing and protective; tough and tender, gentle as well as strong in leadership. But to the man who learns how to handle the tender touch, all the rewards of maleness are his to own. The fellow who can handle all the four types of balls— **Provision, Protection, Leadership,** and **Nurturing**—is no longer a little-leaguer. He has earned a spiritual trophy for making God's all-stars in emotional maturity; He has become a man.

The kind of dad that can pass these four lessons on to his son is an exceptional dad. He is a true Hall of Famer. We will look more at the manhood characteristics of Hall of Fame dads in the next chapter. But for now, let us consider the concept of being fathers to our sons and being sons to our fathers.

If you are a son in this program, you have very little to go on by way of field experience. Your role is like a rookie on a major league team. You are learning to be a dad even at your age. I know that the farthest thing from your mind right now is being a dad. But believe me, you are exactly that. A dad in the making. Your responsibility for the next few seasons is to be a watcher and a catcher. However, that does not mean that you must remain silent. No. Instead, ask all the questions you can think of.

Consider your dad your coach and team manager. Look to him for answers. You already know he does not have all the answers, but he has a lot more than you are giving him credit for. The very fact that you are in this rite-of-passage game is demonstrative of his care for you and his concern for your future as a man.

As for you, dad, yours is a really tough job. You must connect with your son in ways your dad might not have taught you to connect. You are responsible for tossing your boy the types of balls he can catch. You have to know his ability, just how much challenge to give him. What responsibilities can he handle? Plus, you have to hand him the glove to catch with. That is never easy, especially when he is not really ready to be first string yet. Young men need models that are living demonstrations of Bible character, not just words on a page. The basic elements of a godly man's character can be found in the pages of the Holy Bible, but they need to be authenticated in the day-to-day life that a father lives in front of his sons. That is why I believe we need a rite of passage program for young adult males. Where else can modern man turn if not to dad. Without dad's input, the young man is left to the confusion of today's self-centered, sin-crazed world.

The confusing image of the American male is different for every social group. Each ethnic sub-culture has a different idea of manliness. A standard malehood symbol needs be one that has not been previously dictated by a racial or cultural norm. Other-wise, all other ethnic groups would shun it. The standard must be set by time-tested values that cut across racial and cultural barriers. This is exactly what the Bible presents. All the child-rearing principles that fathers need can be found in the pages of the Bible. Plus, there are dozens of good guides to help fathers find the information that is needed to help him direct his children. The fact is, parents have many more resources today than were available twenty years ago. A visit to the local Christian book store can be almost overwhelming as one considers the books and guidelines. However, none are worth the reading if dad does not commit to be a coach, not just a spectator.

Be a Hall of Fame dad. Let ManTracks be your coaching guide and teach your son to catch. Where is your son, by the way? Is he the one in right field?

Reflections …

Respond to the questions below by writing in your own notebooks then discuss the ideas you have written when you are alone together.

Dad:

- How do you feel about being a coach of life?

- Did your dad pitch you some good balls, or did you get some lousy bouncing grounders? Share the truth with your son about the way you feel about your role and ability as a "pitcher" and as a "coach."

- Be truthful with yourself and your son about his ability to take on the four responsibilities we have listed. Take some time to discuss each "ball" with him over the next few weeks (Protection, Provision, Leadership, and Nurturing).

Son:

- How do feel about being a catcher? How, in your own opinion, have you handled the four areas in your life so far?

- What do you think you can do to make your track into manhood smoother in these four areas, that is, what kind of "pitching" do you need from your dad in each of these areas.

CHAPTER 7

Hall of Fame Dads

We were moving to a new residence and I was pack-
ing my garage stuff, when I saw it. A black and
white baseball card of "*The Babe*" lying inside my tool
box. People who know baseball cards have permission to
salivate now. The rest of you probably don't have a clue as
to why the card is valuable and creates an instant need for
an envy check. But for me it holds even more significance
than the collector's value. Let me tell you why that card
brings such emotion.

I got the card when I was twelve years old. I was a
tough little rag-muffin from east Texas who would never,
ever have opportunity to go to a big-league game. The
closest kids like me would ever get to the Baseball Hall of
Fame was a collection of baseball cards of the famous players. I received the Babe Ruth baseball card from some caring adult males who were part of my image of masculinity.

I had set a record for the most RBI's in the Optimist
Club Pony League of 1955. The coaches and leaders of

that men's club wanted to do something nice for the promising little kid from across the tracks. What they did lives in my heart forty years later. The memories that card brings are fading now. I can't remember the names or the faces of the men who gave it to me, but I remember the event. It will be with me forever. It was a fleeting minute of glory for a little boy with few positive memories to work with.

The man who handed me my prize at that banquet so long ago was some other kid's dad. But I thank God for his involvement in the Optimist Club Pony League. He will always be a Hall of Famer to me.

If you and I want to visit real baseball Hall of Famers we must go to Cooperstown. But if we want to see God's Hall of Famers, we can go to the museum of the Bible, Hebrews, chapter 11. As we walk down the corridors of God's hallowed Halls, we see some guys who were real team players. We see men who were great dads. The museum relics we have come to look for in God's Hall of Faith are memoirs of some of history's really good dads. These are men God is proud of. This is like looking at the Lord's private collection of family pictures, framed for us in leather and India ink. What kind of people were they?

To be sure, these folk were not perfect, they all had sin in their lives, they all made terrible mistakes—like you and me, they did things they were not proud of. After all, these are people not angels, they were human beings, members of a fallen race. But *something* about them caused God to say this man, this woman, deserves to be in my museum. That *something* was their faith. *"This is what the ancients were commended for"* Heb. 11:2.

Check it out—Here are some really good dads

There are some really good dads in this place. We are on our way to visit the Abraham booth today, so we won't have time to stop by the Noah display. This fellow, Noah may have made some mistakes, but when it came time to shut the door of the ark, his entire family was inside— even though everyone else in the whole world rejected him. The dads in this museum seem so different than the celebrities we identify with today. Often, we have a hard time defining what a real man is. In fact, when we ask the question "What is a man?" we get some weird answers: listen to what some of our contemporaries say about men: "Men are oppressors to be conquered. A necessary evil that must be tolerated because social annihilation is illegal". Phyllis Diller said that men are "walking wallets." Rosanne Bar says men are "basically useless things that can read road maps."[1]

But that's not what the Bible says. Here, in this imaginary museum, God's Hall Of Fame, we find a heavy hitter like Abraham, a godly man who is one of the best examples we will ever find of a godly dad. We will ask history some questions about him, and we will find in his life a definition of a man God called up from the minors to lead the Dads to a world victory. We take our hats off to this role model for godly dads. But before we do, let's pause for a minute to open the old family album of our mind.

Flip through the pages of your memory until you come to the picture of that really good dad. Maybe he was an uncle or a grandpa, or maybe your own dear old dad. Whoever you have in your mind's eye is someone you admire. He affected your life in some positive way. What are one or two character traits that you could share that define him? Let me give you a couple of examples: My dad's step-father, Pa Copeland was a godly man of integrity.

I would define him as *strength with a soft hand*, or *tough, but tender*. Pa pointed me to Jesus Christ, and for me, that makes him tower over all the men I have ever known. Then, there's Harvey Wallace, my wife's dad. He was an honest, salt-of-the-earth-gentleman, who faithfully served his family all the days of his life; when he died he left a legacy of strength and honor that lives on in his children.

The Character of a Godly Dad

The character traits of the man who makes God's kind of dad include words like integrity, inner spiritual strength, hard working, fairness, and godliness. He is the kind of dad that teaches his son to catch all four male images: provision, protection, leadership, and nurturing. That is the kind of man Abraham was. Here in God's Hall Of Fame we can see why God holds him in such high esteem. His Spiritual strength and his godly life continue to have an influence on the worlds of Judaism, Islam, and Christianity, after more than four-thousand years!

Abraham was a man who would be called "The Father Of The Faithful" because of what God knew about him (See Genesis. 18:19). His very name speaks of father: How important is dad? The word Father (Ab,) is the first word in the Hebrew dictionary. God places a heavy emphasis on the importance of dads. My humble opinion is, you settle the dad issue, and you have solved most of society's ills. What an awesome responsibility! Abraham is called the father of faith because God knew he would be a model dad, and we desperately need models.

So, what was it in Abraham that made him such a good dad? The answer is found in the simple words of Genesis 18:19.

First, *He knew the way of the Lord!* This phrase is used over fifty times in the Bible. It means God's value system,

His way of doing things. There is a right way and a wrong way to do almost anything. Its time we learn that man's way is the wrong way, God's way is the right way. Proverbs 16:25: *"There is a way that seems right to a man," but the end of it is destruction."*

Larry was out with his 15 year-old son Matt, for an early morning run in the redwood forest during a family vacation last year. Matt, was in the lead several yards ahead of his dad, setting a steady pace. Suddenly he came upon a fork in the trail, and without letting up on his stride, he simply glanced over his shoulder and asked, "Which way, Dad?" Larry simply pointed at one of the paths and Matt bolted down the trail his dad pointed to, never missing a step.

"It seemed so natural," Larry told me later, "Matt knows my heart and he knew I would never point him down the wrong trail."[2]

That's what God does for us (Isa. 30:21):

"Whether you turn to the right or to the left, your ears will hear a voice behind you, saying, "This is the way; walk in it."

Our children know which way to go down life's path because the responsible party in their lives has not only taught them, we have trained them in they way they should go.

The Way of the Lord is the way to Life. Jesus, on that last night with his disciples, told them where he was about to go, and He told them that they knew the way. But Thomas said to Him, *"Lord, we do not know where you are going, how then can we know the way?"* Jesus said, *"I am The Way the Truth, and The Life, no one comes to the Father except through me."* So dads, you know the way to go. It is Jesus Christ.

The second thing we find when we look into the Abraham display in God's Hall of Faith, can also be seen in Genesis 18:19. God knew that Abraham would command his children and his entire household after him.

A loving command is not a demand, it means having a servant's heart for your family. When your family knows that you love them, and that you are there for them; when the children see you romancing your wife and placing more interest in the home than in the job, you can command your family and they will follow willingly. On the other hand, when they observe you give them and their mom the cold shoulder, and in the name of masculinity fail to tuck them in at night or listen to their childish hurts; when they see you walk away and never come back, or try to replace your absence with material things, they will grow up with a hole in their heart so large nothing will ever fill it. They will become angry and bitter, but they will not know at what or whom. They will long inside for a strong arm on their shoulder, and not finding it at home, they will seek it elsewhere.

Here in the Hall of Faith, Heb 11:8-10, we have the portrait of God's kind of dad. At the Abraham display, we see:

"By faith Abraham, when he was called, obeyed by going out to a place which he was to receive for an inheritance; and he went out, not knowing where he was going."

A Hall of Fame dad has decided to obey God.

If we want to understand why so many young people are disobedient to authority, we need to look no further than their dads. Certainly there are exceptions to the rule, but in many cases, adolescents have watched parents disobey God's principles of finances, sexual purity, career development, and social interaction. Why are we surprised when they turn their hearts away from home? The next phrase captures another reason why God considered Abraham Hall of Fame material:

"By faith [Abraham] lived as an alien in the land of promise, as in a foreign land, dwelling in tents with Isaac and Jacob, fellow heirs of the same promise; for he was looking for the city which has foundations, whose architect and builder is God."

A Hall of Fame dad leads his family in the ways of God.

Mark well the words *alien and foreign land.* Abraham's mobile home was always on the move, not because he was a near-do-well indigent with wander-lust fever. It was because he realized the temporal nature of this life. Men, we are either aliens or citizens in this present world. From the earliest age, our kids can see where our value system is anchored. We either belong here, and struggle against the elements to be comfortable here, or we have another citizenship that takes precedent. We have made this world our home, or like my grandpa Copeland used to sing:

"This world is not my home, I'm just-a passing through. My treasures are laid up somewhere beyond the blue. The angels beckon me from heaven's open door, and I can't feel at home in this world any more."[3]

Dad, are you at home in this world? I hope not. I hope you are pointing your children to a better city whose builder and maker is God. Abraham did, he had the godly character that made him God's kind of guy. This is not lip service, its not just saying the right words—its not even *going to church,* as important as that is. It is the integrity of heart that causes actions to match words. It is making important promises and keeping them, no matter what. It means being there. Being dependable and being emotionally present. It's teaching the lad how to catch, training him how to be a godly man in an ungodly world.

What did Abraham know about God?

Again, the Genesis text has the answer. It says the Lord would bring about for Abraham what He [God] had promised him [Abraham]. The significance of this phrase is that, like Abraham then, we can trust God, now. He can be depended on to keep His commitments and promises. One promise God has made is that He will save to the uttermost all who will come to Him in faith. He has promised to love you and me unconditionally and help us become the dad he wants us to be. Some men feel they are out of their league with the kind of stuff I am talking about. They think that God, if He exists at all, doesn't care for them. If you are one of them, I pray as I write this that you will accept God's loving challenge to join His team. God promised to repair what you and I have broken in the past. All we have to do is bring the broken pieces to Him and He will begin immediately to restore those relationships. He invites us to come to Him: God's favorite word in the Bible is "Come."

"Come unto me all you who are weary and heavy burdened and I will give you rest" Matthew 11:29-30.

"Come now and let us reason together says the Lord. Though your sins be as scarlet, I will make them as wool, though they were red as crimson, I will make them as white as the new fallen snow" Isaiah 1:18.

That is God's call. The confusing call comes from somewhere else. It is a call the world refers to as real men. Tough sluggers who will play to win at all costs. It is obvious to me that we don't need any more "real men." What we need is for our men to be real—transparent, clear, open men, willing to let us see what they are made of. We need a crop of dad's today who are not afraid to let us see inside them, and hear the sound of a tender *I love you.* We need dad's who will walk in the way of the Lord.

Dads who are steel—lined with velvet. Available to meet the needs of their family.

Where are All the Godly Dads?

Where have all the godly dads gone? It seems they have all left the park before the game is over. It is embarrassing how the male-dominated Christian community has failed to substantially impact the twentieth century western world. If our Christian life were a ball game, we would be having a cellar year! Christian men have basically ignored a crucial social rule, one which has left a generation of coachless players to blast headlong into the twenty-first century with no game plan! Christian men have not provided a collective, specific model to adolescent males for how to become a man.

A rite of passage for Christian males is a non-subject in most contemporary church groups. A historical survey of the last two-hundred years produces an embarrassing blank page under the heading of "Coming of age in the Christian Community." In short, there are no models.

Where are the hall of fame dads today? What was once a well defined model has vanished, blown away with the dust of the Chisolm trail. The super-heroes of yesterday's Gotham City have given way to the less-real characters in space platforms, light years away from our down-home America. Everywhere, men are trying to adjust, looking for a male model. And where else should they find him than right in their own home, with a godly dad and a specific program to help the younger male become a man. A program designed to offer step-by-step assistance for both father and son. In a very real sense, a program such as ManTracks should not be necessary.

Christian culture ought to include rites of passage ceremonies for men and women as an established norm.

After all, have not Christians been at the business of passing the torch to the next generation for almost twenty-one centuries? Yet never before has the model of Christian character been more unclear.

It is no wonder that the Christian life, presented in the pages of the Bible, is virtually extinct. The proverbial blame-finger points to an amorphous pool of guilty souls, collectively called men. Actually the finger points in the right direction. Men *are* responsible for the condition of their homes because men have been virtually irresponsible about the condition of their homes.

We fellows may point at the (not so) weaker sex and complain about feminism, but every man knows the truth. Men have essentially abdicated their position as leaders in the home and in the Christian community. The absence of individual male leadership in the home has left a vacuum too large to be filled by Christian art, literature, or the best efforts of women. What then, can be done? We can begin to empower dads, with truth and positive support, that will be a good start. Does that sound too simplistic? It may not be sophisticated enough for twenty-first century socioeconomic power-brokers, but our real need is for fathers to assume their roles as the real men of today.

A Man's Man Is a Godly Man

Real men are not the celluloid heroes of a plastic-and-mirrors world, dominated by a confusing array of rock stars and ninja kickers. Maybe you have seen the slogan that tells it like it is: "A man's man is a godly man." It is one of the many identifying phrases of Promise Keepers®, the phenomenal men's movement that is sweeping across this land like a refreshing breeze.

Virtually no one can replace a godly dad in the life of a developing man-child in a Christian home. Nearly one hundred years of emotionally inactive or absent fathers has taken a terrible toll on American society. The results of homes without godly male models are blatantly obvious. It would be trite to cite the data on the violent crime rate, increasing over the four generations since World War I. Statistics on immorality, divorce, illegitimate pregnancy, abortions, homosexuality and teen-gang killings are redundant facts of media. Everyone knows, and almost nobody cares. Where are the fathers? One answer is that, beginning with any given generation over the past eighty years, fathers in wholesale numbers have not assumed the responsibility to teach their sons how to become men. Someone has failed to teach our sons that fatherhood does not begin with seminal fluid, that it begins with a relationship with a woman with whom a home is created.

Rebuild the Father Image

That is why we must begin to rebuild the father's image. There has never been a period in the history of mankind that men have been so demoralized as today. I began this chapter with a question, what is a man? Of course there is no single answer. We are a nation of desperate men, trying to fill an empty hole in our hearts. We are men desperately seeking the affirmation and masculine image we were supposed to have received from our dads, but did not. We are a generation of aliens, blindly seeking pleasure, power, material objects and things to conquer because we don't know who we are. Can anything be done to salvage the image of fatherhood, and to place men back in their rightful places of respected leadership in the home and the church?

The first step

The first thing is for fathers, one by one, to make an immovable, unqualified decision to be the father God intended. That kind of commitment can be frightening, especially with the of the lack of father- images available today. It obviously isn't as easy as saying, "Here I am. I'm male, follow me." It involves a total commitment to the Biblical concept of family. The home and family are God's ideas. God designed the family to manage His earth and exercise dominion over all the other creatures He made. The Lord's first command to Adam and Eve was to multiply and replenish the earth. It is obvious that He did not mean to simply manufacture more little children, abandon them and go make some more. Of course not! The clearly evident replenishing process was to be accomplished with more families.

Men must re-establish their God-given responsibility to their family by an unconditional commitment to their children's mother. A man cannot relinquish his responsibility as a husband without damaging his children in the process. The inescapable fact is that children are shaped by the relationship between mom and dad. Men should forget trying to be good week-end dads. That the father can walk out on his marriage and still remain a good dad is one of our society's most hideous lies. Its nearly impossible to be a good *absent father*. It is irrational to expect children to be unaffected by a father who abandons his relationship with their mother. It is downright stupid to believe that an irresponsible father can build a generation of responsible sons. The home is the central building block in the society. One cannot separate fatherhood from the home without destroying both entities in the process. There is no such thing as a casual divorce when children are involved.

The sad fact is that more sons (and daughters) are abandoned by fathers who never established a home at all than by divorce. The almost unbelievable statistic is that there will be nearly one-half million unwed mothers who will give birth to children this year. Most of these women are teenagers who have no way to support their children. Many do not have parents to help them because they are products of the father-abandoned homes, too. If this were not bad enough, over one-fourth of these illegitimate children will be second-born! Eighty percent of them will be adults who were reared without a dad.

The Ugly Two-headed Monster

This condition has become a social monster with two very ugly heads. First, where there is no adult male mold, the clay-like character of a boy will conform to the shape of his strongest external pressure: peers (whose father's have also disappeared). This blind-leading-the-blind problem has no solution, where young men by the multiplied thousands get their understanding of masculinity from television, Playboy, and Madison Avenue money mongers.

Second, when left to become a man in a world without positive male icons, a boy becomes the next generation's absent father. As this spiral continues, with almost genetic accuracy, the results are appallingly predictable. How many more generations will inherit the frightening whirlwind that sowing to the wind has produced?[4]

There is only one solution: This generation must begin the conscious task of character-modeling. Someone has said that more is caught than taught. There has never been a more verifiable reality. Life is a show-me process. Although Christian manhood does have an operating manual—the Holy Bible, a boy can no more learn how to become a man by reading about character, than he could master the rapids by reading a book on canoeing. Many have referred to the Bible as an operations manual, but it was never designed to be a solitary learning tool. The Bible is certainly a tool for learning, but it is the father-to-son process that makes the words effective. Proverbs. 1:1, 2:1, and scores of similar passages indicate the necessity for fatherly input. It is not that the Holy Scriptures are inadequate for single youths to grow from. Unquestionably, Scripture is the most adequate resource available, especially when the young person knows the Author personally, but fatherly involvement is dramatically more effective than leaving a son to learn the Bible for himself. Father-to-son was the Master's design originally, and it still is.

Reflections ...

Respond to the questions below by writing in your own notebooks then discuss the ideas you have written when you are alone together.

- Who comes to mind as a really good dad? What are some characteristics that made him such a good dad?

Dad:

- In the coming months, what attitudes or actions do you want to work on to make your ManTracks program with your son more meaningful for both of you?

Son:

- What things do you need from dad that will make your ManTracks program more meaningful?

- What responsibilities can you take off your dad's shoulders, making his load a little lighter, and enhancing your position as a man?

- What is it going to take for your dad to make the Dad's Hall Of Fame?

PART II

Milestones to Manhood

CHAPTER 8

How to Use the Milestone Guide

Milestones are memory points that punctuate events related to the ManTracks program. They are relational activity and discussion periods designed to address emotional and Spiritual growth for young men. The son in this program is growing, becoming a man—but he has not yet fully grown. When does that occur? In the physical realm, there are some clues of biological maturity. We can see body hair, we can smell body odor (boy! Can we ever!), and we can hear voice changes. We can feel his physical strength and watch his shoulders and chest begin to bulge. These are often the only signs of adulthood that our culture recognizes; yet, these signs do not denote maturity. Physical changes suggest the possibility that he is able to procreate, but we know reproductive ability alone does not make him a father—they do not even make him a "man."

How then can he, or his dad, or his world know when 'maturity' has arrived? When is he a man? The only correct answer lies in a unique combination of physical, mental, emotional, social, cultural and Spiritual factors. ManTracks does not attempt to manipulate the slow, deliberate process God has set into action. The best we can do is document the metamorphosis! Really, that's what ManTracks does.

A Word To Dads...

As a dad, you are helpless to change most of the stuff your son is experiencing. During the six months or so of this program, you will deal with only a microcosm of his maturity. Take advantage of the opportunity you have to record some significant change-points. Check off the emotional and Spiritual elements of each Milestone in the context of a relational bonding experience. In other words, get in there and participate with him.

Never mind that no one ever did this for you. This is for your son—you are responsible to God for his training, he is responsible to God for his attitude and his behavior. Don't get those mixed up! You cannot answer to God for him, but you can influence him in the right way to go by helping him confront some of the strategic issues of life. He has been watching you for several years, learning from you what manhood is.

Each Milestone is keyed to an important Spiritual or emotional development concept, but it must be enacted in an interest-stimulating context if it is to be lasting. If your son does not think its fun, then he will loose interest quickly.

Never forget the reason for this program. You want to assist in his becoming a man. He really is still a boy in many ways. Boys act like boys, not men. It frustrates us sometimes, and we often want to say, "Act your age!" When he might very well be doing just that. So do not think of this as another Sunday school hour. If he thinks you are being just another teacher, cramming some redundant Bible lessons down him, he will rebel.

The best thing you can do is lighten up and be yourself. Let your son see the real you. You don't have to be an unsmiling, somber, crypt-host to be serious. Your son already knows your moods. When your are relaxed, you will be able to get much more from him than when you are tense and melodramatic.

Recording Relational Activities

Time is so short! We just don't have enough time to get everything in. Yet, somewhere in your gut you know that your Creator has given you exactly enough time to do what you should do to be the dad you have been called to be. Often, tough choices have to be made between things we do not wish to give up, and things we must sacrifice in order to invest in the things that are really important. That is why ManTracks has been designed to give you the maximum opportunity to use your time wisely.

We humans forget so easily, life flies by so swiftly; we often need physical memory-joggers to help us recall the good times. This is what God did with Israel in the Old Testament. He commanded them to do specific things that would remind them of how He had blessed them. The entire Jewish calendar is designed around these special events. This is true of our nation as well. Our special event days became holy days, that are memorials of when some important action took place.

These relational periods that you and your son spend together will soon become a warm and precious image in your son's mind of what it means to be a man. The notes you make will live for many generations. The ManTracks Digest, like a family album, will become a reminder of you and his relationship with you every time he looks at it. It will give him the mental and visual images he needs to guide him when he becomes a father. Your son may not think so now, but someday he will take great pride in displaying his ManTracks Digest. So, do everything possible to make these relational times as meaningful as possible.

The form below can help you remember what you did with specific time spent together. For each of the twelve Milestones, write down what you and your son did, when you did it, how long it took, and other basic facts. It might seem redundant now, but forty years from now, when your son is explaining this to his son, he will have a memory jogger.

How we decided what we would do for the Activity:

What did you do? Where did you go? When (Date)?

How do you evaluate the activity? Did you interact by talking to each other? If so, what was your conversation about?

Tell how you felt about being on this activity together.

How did this activity relate to your son becoming a man?

How would two "real men" do this activity differently than you did it with your son? (Try and make each activity seem more like two men doing it together. If we want our sons to grow up, we must treat them more like grown ups).

Did you take pictures? Remember to date them and write a short comment under each one as you put it into your ManTracks Digest. What other momentos did you bring back? Have you put them your ManTracks Digest?

Emotional and Spiritual Emphasis

Each of the twelve Milestones are specifically designed to align the Spiritual Question with the Milestone of that subject in the same section. The philosophy behind the twelve Spiritual Questions is that Christians are a unique community, a family, really, under the leadership of God, our Father. Jesus Christ is both our savior, and our big brother.

Specific Instructions

Milestones are designed to be completed in a relational outing with you and your son alone. Since there are a total of twelve Milestones, and because (ideally) they occur every-other-week, it is impractical for most dads to take their sons on an over-night trip twice each month. This means that some of the Milestones will need to be done close to home. However, the material you will cover in each Milestone will take several hours, so don't try to do this in his room with the TV going! You must get where you can be undisturbed. Here are some suggestions for those times when you cannot go away overnight:

- Take a walk in the park. Sit at a park bench to work on your Milestone.

- Borrow a relative's or a family friend's house for a few hours while they are away.

- Go to a nearby library and check out a 'study room.'

- Use a college or high school campus. (Depending on the date, you could be inside or outside.)

- Stay home while the rest of the family goes somewhere else for a few hours.

Plan to get away overnight as often as possible. Some ways to make this happen is to 'double-up' a family outing. You could go with other people as long as you spend several hours of quality time working on your ManTracks Milestones together.

Getting The Best Use Of The Milestones Questions

Since, as it has been said, Milestones are the heart of the ManTracks program, fathers and sons should each get a simple notebook - like a spiral-bound, ruled notebook - to use throughout the program, for writing down your ManTracks notes and journal entries. Later, prior to your rite of passage ceremony, you will want to transfer some of these notes into a family ManTracks Digest (album) where you will also keep pictures and other memorabilia from your ManTracks program.

The Milestone subjects are designed to get young men to think about and discuss adult-manhood issues with their dad. Fathers are encouraged to stimulate conversation and keep the discussion meaningful. This program is not an all-in-all. It will not make your boy into a man. It will be only slightly more than a time consuming hassle if it is reduced to a "fill-in-the-blanks" procedure. The Milestone questions are intended to stimulate discussion. Talk, men. Learn to express your feelings about one another openly and unashamedly. Be real. This is the beginning step in becoming a man of God.

Spiritual Milestones

The philosophy behind the Spiritual Milestones is that Christians are a unique community, a family, really, under the leadership of God, our Father. Jesus Christ is both our Lord and our big brother. The relationship between the Father and the Son is the perfect example for earthly fathers and sons. Men in God's holy family are responsible for the Spiritual growth of our individual family units as well as being leaders in the community at large. This is a serious responsibility. Women also have specific and mandatory roles, and often these include leadership, also, but there is no denying a man's responsibility in the biblical sense.

Over the past several years, men have placed undue pressure on women by refusing to take the responsibilities the Bible outlines for men. Being responsible citizens in the Lord's community, many women have taken up the slack and stood in the gap when men did not, and they are to be commended for that. Generally speaking, men have lost our way as Spiritual leaders in the past few years. For reasons too detailed to discuss here, men have placed a greater emphasis on provision and protection, than on leadership and nurturing. Now, we are beginning to see a return to the Bible.

In unprecedented numbers, men are seeking guidance and training in the areas of spiritual leadership and godliness. With the help of several national organizations, such as Promise Keepers®, men are being encouraged to take their rightful place in Spiritual leadership. Spiritual Milestones are tools to help you focus on the basics of the Christian faith. They are designed to challenge your son (and you) to examine roles, relationships and responsibilities as men, from a biblical point of view.

This is what God did with Israel in the Old Testament. He commanded them to do specific things that would remind them of how He had blessed them. The entire Jewish calendar is designed around these special events. Jesus followed the same pattern with his disciples. The symbols we hold dear are reminders of his Truth and Way.

When you spend time together, doing your relational activity, you answer the questions and discuss the issues under the Spiritual and Emotional headings and check the box when each MileStone is completed. Below are listed the Milestones in overview. When you complete an activity check it off and get set for the next one. You will appreciate this opportunity to enhance your relationship, once you get into it.

How to Use the Milestone Guide

Milestone 1 ❏   Relational . . . . .Father Son Activity No. 1
Subject . . . . .Filling The Masculine Void
Spiritual Question . .Who made me male?

Milestone 2 ❏   Relational . . . . .Father - Son Activity No. 2
Subject . . . . .Defining Manhood
Spiritual Question . .What can I do with my sin
nature?

Milestone 3 ❏   Relational . . . . .Mother - Son Activity No.1
Subject . . . . .Christian Manhood Values
Spiritual Question . .What is real Christianity?

Milestone 4 ❏   Relational . . . . .Father - Son Activity No. 3
Subject . . . . .Manhood Responsibilities
Spiritual Question . .What is a godly man?

Milestone 5 ❏   Relational . . . . .Father - Son Activity No. 4
Subject . . . . .Manhood and Provision
Spiritual Question . .Why is Communion so
important?

Milestone 6 ❏   Relational . . . . .Father - Son Activity No. 5
Subject . . . . .Manhood and Protection
Spiritual Question . .What godly men do with
violence.

Milestone 7 ❏   Relational . . . . .Father - Son Activity No. 6
Subject . . . . .Manhood and Nurturing
Spiritual Question . .How does a godly man feed
himself?

Milestone 8 ❏   Relational . . . . .Father - Son Activity No. 7
Subject . . . . .Manhood and Leadership
Spiritual Question . .What is a Spiritual Leader?

Milestone 9 ❏ Relational . . . . .Father - Son Activity No. 8
Subject . . . . .Manhood and Family
Heritage
Spiritual Question . .How do Spiritual legacies
happen?

Milestone 10 ❏ Relational . . . . .Mother - Son Activity No. 2
Subject . . . . .Manhood and the Female
Person
Spiritual Question . .What is God's idea of
gender roles?

Milestone 11 ❏ Relational . . . . .Father - Son Activity No. 9
Subject . . . . .Manhood in a World of
Other Men
Spiritual Question . .How does a man stay
accountable?

Milestone 12 ❏ Relational . . . . .Father - Son Activity No. 10
Subject . . . . .Expectations and Realities
Spiritual Question . .What does God want of my
life?

CHAPTER 9

MILESTONE 1

Filling the Masculine Void

Comment On The Following Statements:

"Everywhere you look you can see evidence of young males, desperate to prove their manhood, behaving in ways they think society expects men to act, and in the process, acting more like children than children."

"The most obvious missing ingredient in the Christian community is a coming-of-age ceremony. The lack of a specific rite-of-passage that marks a moment in time when adolescence graduates into maturity has created confusion and doubt in both youth and adults. Every man knows what the unexplainable void feels like. Today, it seems everybody is talking about it, but nobody is doing anything about it."

- What Has The Lack Of A Rite Of Passage Program Meant To Our Society?

- Is There Such A Thing As A Masculine Mystique?

- What Is Your Opinion Of The Following Statement?

"Our culture demands a certain quality in adult males that draws clear distinctions between "boy" and man, and between "woman" and man. This mystique is couched in terms like "valor," "balls," and "macho." It begins in the cradle and doesn't end until the mortuary. In order for men to fulfill their masculine void, that distinction must reside internally, and be expressed externally. But with the lack of positive male icons—masculine role models, young men turn to false images in movies, music videos and other media for their models."

"When wrong external male distinctives are forced inside young males by the pressure of a godless society that is motivated by greed and anger, the results are often disastrous. The father-wound runs deep as confused teenagers try everything from drugs and alcohol to uninhibited sex to prove they are a man. Fathering children becomes a symbol of male virility in many circles, never mind the fact that they have injected abandoned children with a father hunger that will never be fulfilled."

"We need a set of action steps flexible enough to work in any father-son environment. Young men and their fathers could certainly use a male-bonding training manual! A memory-keeping program that guides young men and their dads through a self-paced program that encourages them to put words and action to their relationship, while they addresses many of the important topics of manhood. Such a tool should be designed to help them keep a record of the most significant journey of their lives. Together fathers and sons can produce a "digest," a kind of album to preserve precious moments during a rite-of-passage program. This coming-of-age process will create moments they will remember the rest of their lives. The program would lead to a ceremony where the father blesses the son publicly and announces him a man."

- How Can The Masculine Void Be Filled?

The Spiritual Question

Who made me?

Read Psalm 139 together as father and son. This Psalm offers special insight to a person's Spiritual value and worth. Pay special attention to verses 13-16.

The following questions were designed to help the young man in the ManTracks program see his worth in God's eyes, which will also help him learn to verbalize his value as a man. One of the major problems with men today is a lack of self confidence. This usually stems from a poor relationship with their father. Most Christian counselors agree that this dramatically affects a man's relationship with God. Therefore, a good starting place to discover godly-man issues is right here at this point. Answer the following questions:

- Whose idea was it to bring you into this world? (V. 13)

- According to the Bible, when did your life begin? (V. 15, 16)

- How do you react to the words of Psalm 139:13-16?

- Write in your journal a few paragraphs that you might use in your ManTracks Rite-of-Passage Ceremony speech, about what this Psalm says about your worth as a person.

CHAPTER 10

MILESTONE 2

Defining Manhood

A Special Project For Dads

In chapter 5 we talked about the confusing images men have to live up to today. Go back and look at the "10 Commandments of the American Man." Develop an explanation of each of these ten statements. Develop a *counter-statement* for each of the humorous statements about men. If you need help with this project, ask your pastor, or an older Christian man who has a good knowledge of the Bible and of God's ways. How do you think these rules came to be? How humorous are they, really? Do you understand the subtle implications of each one? Try and explain each one of these to your ManTracks son when you get together to do this MileStone. Make sure he understands the implications of them.

A Special Project For Sons

Using a tape recorder, do a survey of ten different men. Ask five from the non-Christian world and five from different church groups to give you their brief "off-the-cuff" and unrehearsed definition of manhood. Try to get various cultures and ethnic groups involved. This could take some time, but it will be well worth the effort. If you are creative, you can get a good interview from several people at one time—say, in a Bible study, at a sports event or just in the marketplace. Men are generally helpful when it comes to assisting young men in projects. I want to warn you that you may not learn a lot about "what a man is," but you will learn a lot about men in general. Men, you will discover find it difficult to express exactly what manhood is, although all men want to think they 'have it.'

When you have gathered your data, get together and discuss it with your dad. Together, develop your own personal definition of "Manhood," by answering the question, "What is a godly adult man?"

The Spiritual Question

It is imperative that a man growing up in today's society understand the implications of sin and its awful consequences. Even though different church groups teach this subject a little differently, there are several Biblical issues that we cannot overlook. As you become a man, you will be responsible to live and teach the Christian message. What is the Biblical message to men about sin? What is it and what does it do?

Read Romans chapter 3, paying special notice to verse 23. Also read Isaiah chapter 53 and mark verse 6. Finally, read Romans 6 and mark verse 26. The following questions relate to these verses specifically. Your dad and/or your Spiritual leader may want to help you with other passages as well.

- Paul, the author of Romans presents the argument in chapter 3 that Jews and Gentiles are alike under sin. What does he mean by alike? (Compare verse 9 with verses 10-18).

- Who is Paul referring to in Romans 3:10-18? Who is included?

- Explain Romans 3:23 and Isaiah 53:6 in your own words, using personal pronouns.

- What are some ideas about sin that you have heard from the world's point of view?

- What does the word 'death' mean in Romans 6:23? What causes it?

- How many "sins" does it take to make one a sinner?

- What is the result of "falling short" of God's mark?

- What does it make you want to do when you think of yourself as a sinner, standing in front of a holy God

__ Run and hide from God, hoping He is too busy running the world to find me.

__ Repent and pray for mercy, trusting in the payment Jesus made to God for my sin.

__ Rely on my ability to persuade God to accept my religious work to offset any sins I may have committed.

- According to the Bible verses you read for this lesson, and other parts of God's word you have read before, to which of the above choices would God most likely respond positively? Why?

CHAPTER 11

MILESTONE 3

Christian Manhood Values

It is difficult enough for a young man who has Christian parents to find his way in today's valueless society. How much more difficult would it be if you, as a son going through this rite of passage program had no Christian father to lead you? You may think you would do just fine without your dad, but God does not think so. To be a Christian man in today's world, we must have godly values ingrained deeply within us. It takes a daily home life with godly parents for that to happen. You should thank God every day for godly parents.

Special Project For Dads

This Milestone is about values. How do you teach values to your son? You know values are trained better than taught. They are the stuff of life that is caught while growing up in a home. Everyone has a set of values. They may not be very well defined, and they may not line up with Christian standards and principles, but they exist. Ask yourself what values you have entrusted into your son so far. How is he doing with integrity? Do you catch him in many lies, or does he tend to cheat on exams or sluff off on homework? How about his attitudes around the house? Is he learning to be kind and gentle with siblings? To be sure, this is the hardest task of parenthood. Teens can try our patience like nothing else. But we must not throw up our hands and give up. We must not relinquish our responsibility to the school system or to any other organization. The last verse in the Old Testament promises a curse on the land when fathers hearts are not turned into the home (Malachi 4:5). The passage is an excellent platform to explain your responsibility as a dad.

"...and he will turn the hearts of the fathers to their children and the hearts of the children to their fathers..."

Dads, please note three things about this verse. First, fathers are mentioned first, not children. It is your responsibility to turn your heart to your children. Jesus said, "Where your treasure is there will your heart be also." Are your children your treasure? Or is it your job or your own ego? Second, the verse indicates that fathers are the responsible party in this transaction. Notice that mothers are not even mentioned in the verse. Of course mothers have a very important role, but in God's book, he made the dad responsible for setting the spiritual climate in the home. Third, this verse suggest that when your heart is turned toward your children, they will respond with their hearts. That is a promise you can take to the bank. It may seem discouraging now, but just hang in there, doing what God called you to do—with grace and love. God will always keep his promise.

Special Project For Sons

During Milestone 3 you will do a very important thing.. You will ask your mother to go out on a date with you. You will treat her as though she is the daughter of your meanest football coach, and he is watching from across the room. You will treat her as if she is God's daughter (which she is), and He is watching from behind your eyes. You will take her to some nice place where the two of you can talk. The subject of your conversation, among other things will be YOU and your value system. You will give her an opportunity to express in her own terms how she feels about this program, about you and your future as a man, and about values she wants you to work on. Your mother will get the opportunity to show you how grown-up women act on a date. She will also get the privilege of telling you about your birth and about her life as a teenager. She will give you a woman's view on how to treat women and how to relate with them.

Since women are going to be of uppermost importance to you as you get more mature, it stands to reason that the most important woman in your life should have the opportunity to date you and help in your rite-of-passage into adult manhood. Your mother knows more about men than any girl you will date in several years. She has more information in her head and in her heart about you than almost anyone else. Give her an evening to advise you on your value system.

Let Mom Read This

Values are so very hard to teach. The reason is people learn by doing and observing, not just listening. Your son (and your daughters too, of course) have been learning values since they could hear you talk and watch you. They pick up more than we know (more than we want them to!) and we as parents are solely responsible before God for the formation of their values. Even when the enemy of their

113

soul attacks them in the form of well-sounding programs at school, such as "Values Clarification," which got its beginnings in the pits of hell, we still are responsible to help them sort out truth from error. If this were easy, God would have someone else do it. But it is not easy, so He chose you. You and your husband. Together, you fill the biblical norm for training your children in values.

What values are most important? Certainly we cannot do justice to them in a book like this, but you can. You and your husband have been doing a good job. How do I know? Because you are reading this book. You are one in a million. Of course I wish that you were one of a million, out of ten-million, but the point I am making is that you and your husband stand out as leaders because you will take the time to consider this type of program for your son. You are to be complimented and commended. Keep up the good work. However, the values we want to stress in this program deal with your son's integrity, wisdom, moral system, people-relations and his value of himself as God's representative on this earth.

You will want to emphasize his sexual image of himself (who does he think he is, in relation to God, to other men, to women, etc.), and his sexual values. Of course these cannot be covered in this one Milestone, or out on one date with your son. But you can cooperate with your husband as he attempts to take your son through ManTracks. Your united front in this, as in all things will give your son a feeling of stability and belonging.

So as you go out on a date with your son, help him treat you the way you hope he will treat women for the rest of his life. Give him a heavy dose of loving guidance from the female perspective. He is your captured audience for an entire evening. Talk his ears off!

The Spiritual Question

The Spiritual Question for Milestone 3 is "What is Real Christianity?" The question is designed to get you to think of yourself as a man of Christ. As a participant in the ManTracks program, you are constantly challenged to consider your manhood in light of your relationships. The most important relationship you have, that with God Almighty, affects every other relationship in your life. That is why you must begin now to solidify that relationship.

If this program had been written by someone other than a Christian, you might not be confronted with Spiritual Questions at all. Yet, the basis of this program is rooted in your relationship with God through his son, Jesus Christ. If you have never been taught Christian values it will be difficult for you to complete this program. These lessons are merely reminders of your Christian training, they certainly cannot replace it. However, one aspect of your adult manhood is going to be your ability to stand up for what you believe.

I cannot tell you what to believe, I can only assume that your belief system includes basic Christianity. This information will help you capsule these basic beliefs. Naturally, the Spiritual Questions are general, but they do include the most important things most traditional-historic Christian evangelicals hold dear.

What you believe really is important. Basic Christianity insists on the fact that the Bible is the Word of God and that Christians accept it at their basis for worship and service to God. Your particular denomination or church group may express itself differently than mine, but we will adhere mutually to God's Word. Proper interpretation and analysis of His word is always a matter of careful study and prayerful exegesis, but when one lets the

Bible speak for itself, a common reader can usually understand what God has done for us and what He wants us to do for each other.

Your assignment for this third Milestone is to study one of the famous creeds from history. Let your dad choose one, or ask your pastor or minister to help you to choose one. Read through the creed together. Try and rephrase each line in your own words so that you prove to yourself and others that you understand what that creed is saying. Most creeds have scripture verses to substantiate what they say. Look them up in a Bible with modern language, like the New International Version, and read them together as father and son.

Spend some time discussing each concept. For an example, ask the question, how does this creed explain "God?" Do I basically agree with this? Why or why not. Here are some questions to help you with this discussion:

- Who is Jesus Christ?

- What was his real purpose on earth? Did he accomplish it?

- Was He really born of a virgin? Is that important to your faith? Why or why not?

- Have you really ever read the book of John completely through in one setting, or just a few settings? If you have not, you really should consider reading the entire book before you complete this program. It will give you the Bible's view of who Jesus is, what he came to do, and whether he accomplished it. You will have God's word on the matter, which is much better than yours or mine.

CHAPTER 12

MILESTONE 4

Manhood and Responsibilities

Nothing frustrated my sons more than to hear my standard speech on responsibilities. I think they sometimes would rather have had a beating than to listen to that speech. Yet, there is no one thing that epitomizes manhood more than this one word, responsibility. Responsibility and privilege go hand in hand, without responsibility there is no privilege. Life teaches us this from the time we are able to grasp ideas. When parents train their children to be responsible for picking up their own toys and for assuming small tasks around the house, the child grows up realizing the need to be answerable to someone else for their actions.

Every action has a counter action. Every cause has an effect and every action needs to have an accountability factor. Our wise forefathers established checks and balances in our government in order to insure responsibility. Our Heavenly Father also requires an account of us. We must learn responsibility if we are to be citizens who will be entrusted with anything of value.

Son

For this fourth ManTracks Milestone, you will need to show that you are responsible for keeping appointments and doing your assigned work. However, manhood responsibility involves much more than just doing your chores. Responsibility is an attitude. It is one of the most "adult" character qualities you can possess because your responsible attitude guides you from inside. You do not do something, or refrain from doing something because someone is watching over you, making you perform.

When one has responsible character, they do not have to be told to do the responsible thing. Responsibility entails "knowing and doing that which God and others are expecting of me." What is being expected of you? How about when you are alone with your girlfriend, and you both are feeling affectionate and emotionally attached? The way you act in this kind of situation has more to do with you as a responsible man, than you as a "nice guy." Do you depend on your girl to decide when you have gone too far, or do you take control of your own emotions, your own normal sex drive?

Responsible men do not take advantage of their partner's feelings and play upon them for their own selfish motives. Responsible men say "no" to themselves and their lower nature. Only then can one say "no" to drugs or sex, or any other misbehavior. Being responsible is much more than acting out the right behavior. It involves having the right attitude, taking charge of one's own thought process and exercising self-control.

Do you have chores or areas of responsibility which your parents have assigned for you around your home? You will need to show initiative by doing these things, on time, and without being told. Perhaps you have a job now outside the home, to give you some extra income. You have already seen that your employer expects certain things of you as his or her employee. You should not need to be told to do these things more than once. This is such an important area, that your dad will not check off this Milestone until he is convinced that you are learning true responsibility.

Answer the following questions as an intimate discussion between father and son. Do not just "fill in the blanks," but get into the discussion and dig for true feelings. Look for ways to encourage and place high value on the biblical concept of self control.

- How many girls would get pregnant out of wedlock if *every* man was truly aware of his responsibility as a man, and acted in responsible ways toward his girlfriend?

- Who is responsible to say "no" to an ungodly activity? When does that responsibility begin? How is it exercised?

- Does being responsible mean giving up rights to have fun?

- Explain in your own words why being responsible is one of the most important adult character qualities?

- Name the most responsible adult you know. What is it about them that you notice as being responsible.

- Describe the kind of responsible adult you want others to see you as becoming.

The Spiritual Question

In Milestone four we ask the spiritual question, "What is a godly man?" You are asked to answer that question with God's view, which you find in the Bible. A godly man is a man who has given his life to Jesus Christ, he is a man in whom Christ dwells. Interact with the following Bible verses and discuss as father and son the implications of being a godly man.

- According to John 1:12, 13 and 1 John 5:11-12, what is the difference in someone who knows about God, and someone who has received the word of God?

- What is John referring to when he uses the phrase, "*the Word of God*"?

- You have heard John 3:16 quoted all your life. Almost everyone who watches football on TV nowadays sees this verse in the end zone. What does it really mean? Before you answer that question, look up the verse in the Bible. Read it in its context, especially verses 17-20.

- Read Romans 10:13-16. If any man decides to become a godly man, what is the first thing he must do?

- How do you describe a godly man?

CHAPTER 13

MILESTONE 5

Manhood and Provision

Chapter 6, Catching Manhood, outlined four manhood traits that every boy catches from his dad. The first of these is provision. By provision we mean making a living, providing an income for the family. This Milestone is not intended to imply that the manhood characteristic of provision somehow excludes women. Certainly not. What we are doing here is establishing the male-ego concept of provision. Many men are so enmeshed with their jobs they cannot remember the main reason for having a job in the first place. A man's career takes up so much of his physical energy and mental capacity that there is little left to appreciate what has been earned. It has said that we men are often so busy making a living we forget to make a life.

Certainly we are not saying your career is not important. It is. In fact, it is one of the most important decisions you will ever make. It ranks right up there with whom you will marry. But the problem is, when we get so tied up in making a living we cannot enjoy life, what is the point? We cannot pretend that we are in a career for retirement. Only four percent of American males actually retire. The facts are:

10% of men die before age 65.

62% continue to work part-time after age 65, while receiving social security income.

13% are totally dependent on welfare, live in rest homes, or otherwise depend on relatives or others for their livelihood.

11% retire on a combination of social security and company pensions.

Less than four percent retire on a perpetual income that is near what they earned when they stopped working[1]

- Do these statistic surprise you? Why or why not?

- If most men are not really going to retire, what is the motive of their work?

- What does it mean to most men to "make a living?" What about you, what do you think that phrase means?

- Are adult males responsible for bringing home the bacon?

- How does your family receive income? How do you personally see your role as a provider. Stated another way, what does provision mean to you?

A Father—Son Project

Visit a career guidance counselor together. If you (as a son in this project) are not sure about your career goals let the counselor advise you as to how to go about deciding. Discuss the visit. What did you learn?

The Spiritual Question

What does the Bible say about a man being the provider of his home? How does the well-balanced adult male view this spiritual dimension of his life? Look at Colossians chapter 3. This is one of the most well known passages of scripture on working and the attitude a Christian needs in the workplace. Also read Ephesians 4:28, 1 Thessalonians 3:10-12, and 1 Timothy 5:8.

• What do these verses tell us about provision.

• What is your conclusion on the matter?

• How will you order your life and take control of your future so that as a man, you have a balanced approach to provision?

CHAPTER 14

MILESTONE 6

Manhood and Protection

When we discussed the concept of protection in chapter 6, we used the analogy of a right fielder catching a ball. We indicated that the male characteristic of protection could be represented by the smooth grounder because it is a rather easy ball to field. Do you agree or disagree with the following statements, please answer why, or why not.

- The characteristic of protection is This is perhaps the very easiest ball to field.

- Protection is a male thing.

- Men are usually willing and ready to get our stick and go check on the sounds that go bump in the night and everyone knows that killing spiders is coded in the male's genetic DNA. In fact, one of the growth traits that men hold dear is that time in life when we are no longer afraid of the dark. Many people believe that part of becoming a man is sleeping without a night-light!

- Why are men so protective of their possessions?

- What do you think is behind the social and cultural idea of police uniforms and special markings on the side of police cars?

- Why do we need so much protection?

- Do you think of yourself as a "warrior-protector?"

The Spiritual Question

The spiritual question for Milestone 6 is "What do godly men do with violence?"

- Why do you think violence is more associated with men than with women?

- Is violence a man thing? Have you ever heard of a home for battered husbands?

- What should godly men do when confronted with violence?

- Look at Romans chapter 12:12-20. The Apostle Paul wrote about violence, but not as a core issue. We must take our theology of violence from inferences.

- What did he say?

- Do you consider these to be suggestions, or commands of the Lord?

- What is at the root of violence?

- Why must some men think they can prove their manhood by acts of violence?

- If they would listen to you, what would you tell them?

- When you are angry enough to hit someone, what should you do?

- Do some people deserve to be treated violently? Why or why not?

- How can you explain the violence of the Old Testament? Is God secretly into violence? Does He want the strongest, most physical person to win?

- Lets say you are teaching a group of Junior-high school boys. How do you counter the hundreds of images they receive every day that violence is justified when it is meted out by the right person? (If it is a cop, going after a drug dealer then surly it is OK for the police officer to rough-up the bad guy, isn't it? What if you are going across the parking lot at night with your mother and your sister and a gang attacks you. Is it OK then to be violent in self defense?)

- When is violence OK?

These are hard questions. Each case must be dealt with individually. We use wrong thinking when we attempt to apply a blanket rule of "right or wrong" to some things. God has very directly said "Thou shalt not" to some things, others however have looser boundaries. There is no way to state ahead of time whether you will or will not use some form of violence to protect yourself or your loved ones against evil doers. It is necessary as a Christian, however, to have a policy on this matter. The overriding principle can be found in Paul's admonition to the Corinthians in 1Corinthians 16:13-14. *"Do everything in love."* Adult men need very much to abide by this principle.

CHAPTER 15

MILESTONE 7

Manhood and Nurturing

We used the baseball illustration with the word nurturing, also. We said nurturing is the very worst kind of ball for our right-fielder to try to handle. It is represented by the crazy hopping grounder. "Just about the time you think you have it in your glove, zoom, it bounces up over your head, or to the right or left." The crazy hopping grounder—like nurturing is really tough for a man to learn to handle. Do you think it is true that many fathers never learned the art of nurturing?

Just what do we mean by nurturing. What is it anyhow? Do you agree or disagree with this statement:

"Nurturing seems feminine, but to the man who learns how to handle the tender touch, all the rewards of maleness are his to own."

- What is the tender touch?

- What adult male comes to mind when you think of nurturing? Why?

Some men think it is not manly to show tenderness. What do you think?

Nurturing is a characteristic every adult human being ought to possess. Nurturing should not be misunderstood as nursing. To nurture is a word that means to train or teach. It is one of the words I based this entire course upon. If you were in the first century AD and you were a school-aged boy, you would be nurtured. The Greeks had a term for teaching, training and applying proper discipline to the child. The term was "paideia (pronounced 'pahee-di'-ah). It is a word that can be directly translated into our language using the word "tutelage" or "education."

You will see the term I originally used for ManTracks, Pai-Charis, throughout this book. I made up the term using the idea of nurturing in grace. The Greek term for nurturing was a common term in ancient Mesopotamia, Greece and Rome. They used it to imply training; and disciplinary correction. It was also commonly used in the training of domestic animals, such as horses, where tenderness as well as a strong hand was often necessary. Nurturing is the process of careful training that includes discipline, chastening, instruction and guidance. Unfortunately, the term has become corrupted over the years so that today, nurturing seems like a female thing. But that is not the real meaning of the word.

- How can we develop a better use of the idea of nurturing?

- In the Reflections at the end of chapter six, I suggested that you do a baby-sitting job for a relative or close friend, so that the two of you can appreciate the need to nurture a child for one evening. Have you done that? Will you?

- As an adult man, what will be your attitude toward nurturing? When do you think the adult male no longer needs nurturing?

The Spiritual Question

The Spiritual question for Milestone 7 is "How does a godly man feed himself?"

This is not a trick question. Mature men sometimes do not feed themselves with the nourishing benefits of God's word. They often do not feed themselves with mind-stimulation and emotionally satisfying situations. Being a man, they think all that is feminine stuff. They think there is just no time left after pouring themselves into climbing the corporate ladder, and being involved in sports to think about the cultural aspect of living.

Everyone loves James Bond, the 007 hero of the fiction espionage. He is the man's-man image many men are hung up on. They will only wear a tux if they can unzip a wetsuit and step out of it first. Then, being perfectly dressed and non-wrinkled they step into a high class night club, where they win-big time at their favorite game of chance. They always get the girl and they always beat the odds, never getting as much as a piece of lint on their tux.

While you know certainly that this is pure fiction, nevertheless, the image stays with you. Deep inside somewhere, you think of cultural events in the negative sense. You are inundated on all sides to think of women as cultural and men as backward. Women like the finer things of life, men want beer and pretzels. This image has hurt you more than you realize. It has so stereo-typed your maleness that you are almost uncomfortable in a performing arts role or participating in a modern dance class.

What does the Bible have to say about all this? First, it is important to note that if you looked up the word nurture in a trusty concordance, your Bible would cough up only one passage from the New Testament. It is Ephesians 6:4. Other forms of the word do appear elsewhere, as in Paul's first letter to the Thessolalonians, chapter 1. See what he says in verse 7, and verse 11. Here Paul says he was among them as a nursing mother, kind and gentle; and like a loving father he exhorted and encouraged them.

Read Ephesians 6:4.

- What stands out in this verse as good advice? What is it?

- How can this concept be applied in the home?

- What would you like to see changed about the way your father disciplines you?

- How do you want to discipline your children?

- At what age do you think children should be able to make their own decisions regarding where they go and what they do with their time and energy?

- Where does this idea come from?

Progress Check:

You are approximately half-way through the ManTracks program. How are you feeling about the program so far? How are the two of you communicating? Are you doing more than filling in blanks? Have you purchased an album to use as your "Digest" to hold all your pictures and other memories in? Have you taken pictures?

What plans have you made to get ready for your rite of passage ceremony. Sneak a look at the back of the book. There are helps there to guide you. If you or your father need help with this course, please call us at the number listed in the appendix. We are here to help you.

CHAPTER 16

MILESTONE 6

Manhood and Leadership

Once again we come to the baseball analogy. The poor right fielder in chapter six is being picked on a lot, but we are learning from him, aren't we? The manhood characteristic of leadership is also a difficult ball for us to catch. One reason may be that we think leaders are born, not made. We may erroneously think that only the specially educated or trained person can be a leader. What can we learn from our right fielder about catching the leadership ball?

We said in chapter six that the male characteristic of leadership could be illustrated by the blazing direct hit, which we know can be a right-fielder's worst nightmare. "The blazing direct hit zooms past the infield at speeds over 90 mph—it's about face-high and you either try to catch it or duck!" A man who develops the characteristic of leadership is, like the right fielder who catches the blazing direct hit, only doing what he should do as a man, right? Isn't it true that although we have no training for the job, every man is supposed to "wear the pants in the family." If he does not, he is like the right fielder who ducks to keep from being hit by the ball. What do you think is meant by

"If he misses, it will continue all the way to the right-field fence, for a ground-rule double. How embarrassing!"

Do you agree or disagree with the following statement from chapter 6?

"The idea of being the leader of the family does not mean being a dictator, being mean, or being dogmatic. It does mean looking further down the road to see where a particular decision will end up."

A group of my students at San Jose Christian College, developed a definition of leadership during their course of study in The Biblical Characteristics of Christian Leadership. What do you think of it?

"Leadership is the ability to explain a vision in such a way as to give others a clear enough picture that they can translate it for themselves without loosing its meaning; and it is the ability to empower others to use their gifts and talents to accomplish the vision."

The problem with defining leadership is that it is illusive and dynamic. Although it is a specific skill that can be trained, leadership is a talent that some people have an easier time with than others. The many different styles of leadership can leave the impression that one type is the right type and another type is the wrong type. Don't believe it.

Every man has the responsibility to lead his family in spiritual matters, being a benevolent autocrat with a strong arm and a tender touch is very important to a family. Children need to be told what to do, while teenagers need to be told that they can do. The security provided by a godly dad when he sets good boundaries is not always appreciated, but it is always needed.

Steven Covey is noted as having said "leaders concern themselves with doing right things, while managers want to do things right."[1] Because of this basic difference, many people misunderstand leadership. Every man was called by God, and empowered to be a leader. The kind of leadership I am referring to is a take-charge kind of attitude that requires love and sensitivity toward others, combined with the need to be tough. Being tough does not mean being gruff or rough. There is no place in the home for crude and mean, overpowering bullies. Leadership is not bullying. It is leading. To lead one must be out front. Much like you cannot push a string, but you can pull it, so you cannot push people to get anything accomplished. People like to be asked to follow your lead, especially little people.

Are you ready to answer for yourself why most "right fielders" have a pretty hard time with this ball?

What do you think I meant when I wrote, "We see most of them chasing it, and chasing it, and chasing it."

The Spiritual Question

The spiritual question for Milestone 8 is "What is a spiritual leader?" The question should be addressed in terms of Christian manhood, not in terms of ordaining a minister or an elder. The character traits should be nearly the same, but the idea is to consider every man who is in Christ as a leader for his own life, ministry situation, or his home. It is as J. Oswald Sanders said "It is a general principle that we can influence and lead others only so far as we ourselves have gone."[2] The leadership to which we refer in this Milestone is the leadership of influence. Study the characteristics of a Christian leader from the Bible in Titus chapter 1 and in 1Timothy chapter 3. Discuss the following questions about your own leadership potential.

- Make a list of all the characteristics of spiritual leadership in these two sections of Scripture. Place a check mark beside those that a non-vocational Christian leader could get along without.

- From the remainder, form a definition of the leader's moral habits.

- From the list, form a definition of the leader's maturity.

- How do you line up with this list? As you know, none of the characteristics are to be seen like plucking the pedals from daisies. He has it, he has it not, he has this one, he does not have this one. Rather it is a matter of degree of maturity in that characteristic that determines the leader's potential.

- If you were God, and you wanted to demonstrate a godly man to the world around him, what characteristics would you give him? Why?

- Who do you know who has these character traits? What is his family background?

- Does it stand to reason to you that someone who has good Christian training at home has a better opportunity to lead others than someone who came from an ungodly home?

CHAPTER 17

MILESTONE 9

Manhood and Family Heritage

Why is family heritage important to the concept of becoming a godly man?

Our fathers handed down their social, cultural and Spiritual heritage to us. We received it in the context of a family unit. Some of us came from large, open family groups, others from small intimate ones. In this session we discuss our cultural and Spiritual background. We make connection with the "way we were raised" to the way we want to see our children grow. The basic connection is in the area of family rituals. These can be informal, like the way we open presents at Christmas time, to the way we celebrate birthdays. The how is not as important as the what. We make connection with our past through rituals. For this reason, it is very important for a man to know his Spiritual heritage. It gives him a sense of belonging and continuance. Traditions help us feel secure and permanent. This may be why mankind has always had ceremony and public display of various kinds.

Puberty Rituals

Boys and girls are different! Girls have a built-in puberty rite that boys do not possess. The changes in a girl's body that accompany menstruation are visible and predictable, and manifested externally—from the inside out. Although it may be advisable for young women to participate in a coming-of-age ceremony, it is not necessary. For girls, the ritual of menses is draped on them, as a rite of passage into womanhood, whether they want it or not. Not so with young men. There is no real evidence of when physical maturity occurs in the male species. Boys require intervention from the outside in, to mark this passage. We need to have something happen to us to physically move us out mother's authority and puts us completely into the kingdom of men.

Many primitive societies had puberty rites that provided young men with tutoring and guidance through their manhood passage. These passages offered opportunity for training in manly ways and opened boyhood eyes to a world beyond themselves. In primitive Hopi Indian tribes, old men would allow the rite-of-passage youth to sit with them in their story circles. The old men's tales and stories would illustrate what it meant to be a man in that society. Over many days, in some cases up to several months, the young men would eat, sleep and live in an isolated village with the old men.

Out of these rituals, and ceremonies a boy would develop the attributes of stamina, bravery and heroism, the qualities he would need to be a hunter-provider, warrior-protector, and family leader.

Almost every society had some means of perpetuating this ideal. Many such rituals followed families into their immigration, but were lost in America following the industrial revolution. As the various family heritages disappeared, and the idea of a rite of passage faded, the concept of guiding young men through time-consuming rituals seemed to disappear also. Now, in the absence of clear initiation rites, our society has turned to other kinds of rituals. Some of these rituals are unhealthy for young adults. Many of the natural, one-time events leave young men devastated and guilty. Fraternity hazing can leave scars and shame that last a lifetime. Military boot-camps, designed to "make-you-a-man-or-break-you" leave unrealistic ideas for what it means to be a man. Sports and athletics can be an engulfing and demanding image for youngsters to measure up to. Where is a boy to find the monitoring and character-modeling that he needs to give that external visual for the internal changes that he must make?

The answer is in the relationship with Dad. Fathers in the ManTracks program provide the guidance their son needs. The actual ritual is not as important as the fact that one is established. It does take time, and yes, cooperation between the boy and his dad is a must, but it can be done.

For Dad Only:

Think back over your past, looking for positive and negative rituals in which you participated as a boy. Did you ever build a tree-house or 'fort' with other boys and make up a set of rules by which your little kingdom would function? Did you ever make a sign that said "No Girls Allowed?" Can you remember a military boot-camp or the tough athletic training you endured in order to be accepted?

The idea of this exercise is for you to begin to explain the meaning of rituals to your son. As you write in your journal, realize that the purpose is to provide you with a tool by which you share yourself with your son. Write details that are intimate enough to touch your inner

143

privacy, but appropriate for sharing. Your son is a candidate for adult manhood. He needs to establish some rituals *with* you that will silently shape his thinking. You want to surround your son's inner character with mental images of honor, duty, strength and purity; but in addition you want him to be able to tap into those manly characteristics of courage, bravery, fearlessness and warriorness that are also gifts of God. You can assist in this process by using negative as well as positive examples from our own life. Respond to the following points by writing in your journal, then get alone with your son and discuss each one.

- How do I feel about being a mentor to my son? How was it with your dad, how about the heritage he received from his dad?

- Some rituals that I remember participating in, and what they taught me (both good and bad)

- Some things I would like to see my son and me do to establish our own private rituals.

- Some rituals I want to encourage my son to avoid

The Spiritual Question

The Spiritual Question for Milestone 9 is "How do Spiritual Legacies Happen?"

The best answer for that question comes in the form of rituals that are passed from generation to generation. A ritual can be something simple, like going out as a father and son on the first day of hunting season, or it may be complex, like the Passover Feast. A ritual is an event that happens once and a similar event, marking an important moment, can be repeated over and over. God's covenant people, Israel had many spiritual events that were passed down from generation to generation as stories. The events only happened once, but the stories and meaning of those events lasted throughout the ages. God commanded His people to remember events like the exodus from Egypt—and the Jewish Passover is the result of that memorial. Jesus told His disciples to remember their last supper together, which He said would be a memorial to His death for us. In the same way, ManTracks is an exercise in the special relationship between a father and a son, memorializing the simple events surrounding the young man's rite of passage program.

In Milestone 9 you will accomplish three things:

Look back over the study material you have completed together and make sure everything is complete, with all previous Milestones checked off.

Complete this lesson on the facts and events of the Last Supper. The goal is to truly understand the meaning of taking Communion with the Body of Christ, His Church,

Take Communion together, as father and son, making this an extra special event (a ritual) whereby you identify together, as father and son with God the Father,

God the Son, and God the Holy Spirit, and relating your individual family with the Family of God.

- Read the Gospel accounts of the last supper: Matthew 26:1-2

"When Jesus had finished saying all these things, he said to his disciples, 'As you know, the Passover is two days away— and the Son of Man will be handed over to be crucified.'"

- Reminder, the Passover was kept every year by the Jews. It was first instituted by God Himself in Exodus 12: 14. *"And this day shall be unto you for a memorial; and ye shall keep it a feast to the LORD throughout your generations; ye shall keep it a feast by an ordinance for ever."*

Background verses for the study: The Event: Matt. 26:17-30, Mark 14:12-26, Luke 21:7-2

The Bible study concerns the specifics of 1 Cor 11:23 - 26. Follow these verses as you work together on this lesson. Be sure to observe the following points:

- The words of Jesus to His disciples as he established this holy ordinance of the Church are easily understood. The disciples knew that Jesus spoke in symbolic language of the bread as His body and the fruit of the vine as His blood. The literal presence of Jesus was evident. The supper would serve as a memorial that God Himself secured man's redemption, through the suffering of the incarnate Christ (the bread) and the shedding of His blood (the cup), in vicarious atonement. The Jews remembered their deliverance from Egypt in the annual Passover festival (Ex. 12:24-27).

- Jesus died at Passover time as the new Passover Lamb through whom believers are delivered from sin and Satan. As the Savior ate the Last Supper during the Passover and just before He died, He instituted this memorial of His death. When He said, "This is My body," as He held the bread, the disciples understood the symbolism because they could see His physical body present before them. The Mid-Eastern world considers eating together a sign of the bond among those present, and the Lord's Supper points to the bond among the various people present, and between each participant and the Lord.

- The actions in the Supper express the symbols. The Lord, hands His people the broken bread, saying by this action, "Look! My body was given for you; I died for you." As we Christian take the bread and eat it, making it part of ourselves, we say by this action, "Yes, Lord! You died for me, and I am again showing my response to Your death. I am relying upon You to save me. I renew my vow of obedience to You. I love You." The same goes for with the fruit of the vine.

- Fathers and sons should make sure that there is no unconfessed sin between them, or between self and the Lord before coming to the Lord's Supper. The Supper is for repentant sinners who have put their faith in Christ. It is to be taken seriously, the participants being conscious of the presence of Christ at His table, and not despising others who are present; for they, too, are His body.

- The Lord's Supper is shared "till He comes;" it looks forward to the Lamb's Supper (see reference Rev. 19:7-9).

- In summary, the Lord's Supper is designed to symbolize and communicate five distinct concepts. They are:

   (1) Communion is a memorial. It remind us of the central truth in Christianity—the atonement of Christ (*"...as often as you eat this bread and drink this cup you show forth his death until he returns."*)

   (2) Communion is a celebration of the fellowship of Christ's body (communion of the Saints).

   (3) Communion is a time specifically set aside for the believer to exercise self examination, to confess and repent of any sin, and enjoy full relationship with Christ.

   (4) Communion is a picture of the feast of Passover, symbolizing how He has passed over our sins, bringing salvation.

   (5) Communion is a public proclamation of hope that is in the gospel.

As part of this lesson, you should arrange to share communion together before the next Milestone. Get alone together and pray a prayer of thanksgiving for your individual salvation, and for your relationship as father and son.

CHAPTER 18

MILESTONE 10

Malehood and the Female Person

Plan Ahead For This One!

I trust you can plan ahead for a week-end, over-nighter, or at least a long day alone together to have this discussion. Much can be accomplished if you are alone, and if you have established the intimacy in your relationship that I hope you have by this point in the program. The subject of women, and by default, "sex," is by far the most important topic on a young man's mind. It will go best for both of you if you have your work sheets or notebooks handy to write, read what you have written and talk openly. Bring along the best book you can find on physical anatomy and sex facts. You should already have such a book in your family library. If you do not, talk to your doctor or a good Christian counselor.

Yeah! Finally We Talk About Women...

This is the Milestone you have been waiting for, right? I hope you will not be disappointed. This is among the most important subjects you can investigate during your ManTracks journey. Not that you do not already have all the answers. Beginning a discussion on the topic of sex reminds me of that tried and true story of the man who wanted to have that proverbial 'birds and bees' talk with his son, only to have the son say, "Sure we can talk, dad— what did you want to know?" Its true. Most dads have no idea what their fourteen, or fifteen year old sons know about sex. There are a lot of assumptions that we have about "sex talk" that come from almost a century ago. The ideas are outdated and shallow, still we rely on them. Why is this subject so hard for men to discuss as fathers and sons, and so easy in the locker rooms with other men or boys?

It doesn't have to be difficult. It can be enjoyable, informative and spontaneous. The most important thing in the entire process is BE HONEST. That means dealing with facts. Not commentary on the issues, not moral rules and guilt trips. Its time for a Dragnet command: "Just the facts, 'ma'am, just the facts." The point is, if young men have facts to deal with, they can make rational and intelligent decisions. If what they have to work with is myth and misinformation, even if from the right motive, they cannot make proper decisions.

Young men on their way to manhood must have truth. Fathers, you can trust your training, and you can trust the Holy Spirit to do his own personal work in your son's life. Sons, you can rest in the power of the Holy Spirit to guide you into all truth, and to support you when you stand for what you know is right. Choices you make regarding your relationship with women and your attitude about women affect almost every other area of your life. So making right choices is essential. However, it is your right to make the choices, not your dad's or any one else's.

Let's say we are playing football and I am the quarterback. You bring in a play from the bench, I want to try something else, but I don't tell you, the wide receiver about it. You run the route you were given from the bench. I drop back and throw to the area I had in mind, but didn't tell you about. What will happen? According to the late Paul Bear Bryant, three things can happen, and two are bad! There is not a real good chance that you will catch a pass thrown at the other side of the field. I'll ether get an incomplete, or an interception.

What went wrong? I threw a perfect pass. You were out of position, running the "wrong" route. But wait. You were not running the wrong route, you were running where you were told to run. I threw to the wrong side of the field. Well, this is not such an absurd illustration as you might think. The problem is not a matter of who was running the wrong play. Both plays, under different circumstances could have resulted in positive yardage. The problem is that we were running two different plays, at the same time. That can only result in disaster. And so it is with your relationship with women. If you have misinformation, no matter how "good" you think your macho image is, you will fail with women. Misinformation can only hurt you. Get the facts, then you have a better chance.

There is at least one fact you must know. *Men will never understand women.* Got it? Great. Now we can proceed. The first thing the two of you should do is open the discussion on a physical basis. When you are both sure that son understands the physiological and anatomical differences in the sexes, the real discussion can begin.

It is critically important to start with the brain. Men and women are not just shaped differently, we think differently. You may have been taught in a high school sociology class that we are basically the same, but you did not get that in a graduate course on anatomy. The female brain is wired differently. Get it? Great. These are some biological facts: She can process more data in the same time period than you can. She thinks bi-laterally, that is she uses both hemispheres of her brain simultaneously. You think linearly, meaning you use only one side of your hemispheres at any given nanno-second. Yes, men do have larger muscle mass, but we have less gray-matter per square centimeter than women.[1]

Until you realize that the hormonal changes, which occur every twenty-eight days or so in a woman's body, are responsible for her different moods on any given day, you cannot begin to understand the differences in the sexes. Women are affected by these hormone changes in ways that we men will never really understand. I write these words, and you read them, but according to the women in our lives, we still don't get it! The best we can do is admit that, and ask them to exercise patience with us as we attempt to serve them and love them just as they are.

To Stimulate Your Discussion

Read and discuss the following story told by Frank S. Pitman in his book, "Man Enough." Express what feelings and what thoughts this story evokes:

"George, a friend of mine who used to play fullback for the Cleveland Browns, weighed 230. His mother, a Czech immigrant, weighed only 110, but she still believed she should be taking care of her little boy. Once in a game when he was returning a kick-off, he was hit head-on and knocked out. He came to looking into the face of his little mother in a babushka leaning over him on the fifty-yard line. She said pleadingly, in Czech, "Buddy, is my baby all right?" George snapped to, and with great embarrassment, said, "Mom, you can't be on the football field." To which his mother slyly replied, "But I am here." Dr. Pittman ads, Mothers will always be where their children are needed."[2]

The point of Dr. Pitman's story, and the idea he purports in his book is that men must break away from their mothers in order to become a man. They [men] need to see themselves as independent, not needing mother, who all his life has supplied his every need. At the same time, it is risky outside the protective sphere of her influence, so he seeks a substitute mother. Another "mother" [a woman] to take care of him and meet his emotional needs. He has no better sense at this time in his developing manhood, however, than to misinterpret his emotional need to be mothered. He is going through the toughest time of his life, puberty. His hormones are going wild, so it is only natural for him to think in terms of connecting up with this new "mother" in a sexual way.

There are only three things wrong with that theory. First, it leaves God completely out of the picture, assuming we are evolved animals with only a social conscience to control our behavior. Second, it is based on a Freudian psychological theory that has been outdated since Carl Rogers and Rolo May, both with opposing views, discredited Freud's notion of mother love/mother hate. Third, it offers a non-sin based theory for why we act the way we do. In short, it is a cop-out. We men do not need more cop-outs, we need more courage to believe the Bible and obey God's command.

During mating years, which is almost every waking moment of a man's life after he is twelve years old, men are turned on to women. Temptation is real. The desire to circumvent God's law and His best for us is a constant temptation. It will always be with us. Men were made to mate with women, but we were created in God's image and given His spirit. We need our sex drive to obey his command to procreate and fill the world with righteous humans. But because of the fallen nature we have inherited from Adam, we cannot keep on track to God's command that we connect up with only one woman for life. We have gone haywire and society wants to re-wire us their way. We place guilt on ourselves for even wanting to be connected with the opposite sex, and we blame women for their seductive ways (don't they know how weak we are?).

Consider one more statement, this one by your author. Again, what is your opinion?

"Notwithstanding the above misguided theory, when a boy goes through puberty the anxiety between him and his mother rises because he is becoming a man and he wants to leave her protective clutches. At the same time, he is not yet a man, and the boy in him wants to stay with mother. This tension grows even stronger when the head of the house does not notice him. If dad continues to ignore junior's antics, he will crank up the volume until dad does pay attention. The reason for this is that he must be reassured that this is home. The boundaries exist and he can retreat into them until he is finally able to overpower them and break out.

Fortunately, in normal homes this occurs just about the same time he experiences one of the few rituals he is allowed in public, his graduation from high school. Sometimes a ritual of getting him off to college follows, but often it does not. Now he is free to pursue a relationship with a person of the opposite sex without anyone looking over his shoulder. However in a dysfunctional home environment, where there is no father love and no boundaries to support his need for security and order, a young man will break out as an escape. He will seek acceptance and love, but will re-define these needs sexually. From his first bungling exploit he will continue to use women to meet his own needs until such time as he comes face to face with the truth of his own nature. His only hope is to repent and turn to God who created men and women. If he does surrender to God he will find peace through the satisfying relationship that comes only from knowing God. Only God can satisfy his need for love, acceptance and security."

There is no way a single module in a program like this one can do justice to this subject. It is too large, too encompassing. This woman-man thing is something that must be settled in the spontaneous living of life in the context of a home. Father. Mother. Son. Daughter. Home. There must be a visual, a living model of what a woman is, and how a man is to treat her. These visuals come from mother, from aunt and from older (even younger) sisters. In the day-to-day living in the context of home, a man learns how to act in front of a woman. We must never give in to the notion that there is androgenity or unisex. Men are not superior to women. Women are not superior to men, but we are different. God made us that way and we will always be that way. As father and son, alone in the privacy of their relationship discuss such things as premarital sex, homosexuality, heavy petting, male genitalia, female anatomy, the ways and means of being with women and so on and so on, you alone will be able to determine your values.

A Project For Sons

My suggestion at this point is that you take your mother out on another date. Get real and talk about some of these issues with her. Listen to her point of view, then re-discuss it with dad. Talk, talk, talk. Discuss these issues of man, woman, sex, morals and values until they become almost boring. Why do I suggest such a thing? Because there can never be too much (real) communication. Young men have more to learn than they can absorb in one puberty season. It is unfortunate, but true that you will begin to understand about the same time your grand kids get married!

NOTE: This is a good time to discuss the date for your Rite Of Passage Ceremony. Talk with everyone involved, mom, dad, inlaws, ex-inlaws, step-parents, etc., and set the date as soon as you think you will be ready following MileStone 12 (for more information, see chapter 21 and 22).

The Spiritual Question

The Spiritual Question for Milestone 10 is "What is God's idea of gender role?"

To kick off this session, lets begin with Genesis 1:27 and Galatians 3:28:

"So God created man in his own image, in the image of God he created him; male and female he created them" Gen. 1:27, NIV.

"There is neither Jew nor Greek, slave nor free, male nor female, for you are all one in Christ Jesus" Gal. 3:28, NIV.

When God created man, he also created his sexual counterpart, woman. These two beings are equal in God's eyes as His image-bearers. Together they have an equal position, and an equal purpose in God's universal plan of redemption. Scripture is specific on this point. The equality of the sexes is established on the basis of our spiritual beings, that is to say, the "image of God" is spiritual, not physical. Not all evangelical theologians agree on the interpretation of this point, but we cannot shrink from taking a position on this important issue. Today, the church is dividing over the gender issue. Ministers and entire denominations have taken rigid stands on either side of the line. The most important thing for you as a budding man is to know what you believe and why.

The battle over interpreting the meaning of the equality of the sexes as a subject has created a great inequity in our relationship as sexual beings. Paul, in his letter to the Galatians faced this issue squarely, and so should you. Equal beings before God, different roles in the world is how I take Paul's teaching in Galatians. How do you see it? A safe, and I believe healthy, position on this subject is "equal personhood, different in role and function." Consider the subtle hints given us in Ephesians 5:22-25.

The divinely defined relationship between men and women in their roles as husband and wife is a picture of Christ and the Church. A relationship between God the Father, Jesus who is God the Son, and the Holy Spirit who is God the Body in implied. This is a perfect picture for us as a family. Each is equal, but each has a separate and different function. Neither is better than the other or inferior, each is equally responsible to God for her or his attitudes, behavior and spiritual response. Each is responsible for the way they relate to and treat each other.

May God grant you grace as you work this out for yourself. There is a good passage of scripture for us to end this session on. In Proverbs 30:19 God reminds us of the mystery of this of this ancient problem.

"There are three things that are too amazing for me, four that I do not understand: the way of an eagle in the sky, the way of a snake on a rock, the way of a ship on the high seas, and the way of a man with a maiden."

CHAPTER 19

MILESTONE 11

Manhood in a World of Other Men

Every boy has his favorite super hero. Every super hero has some things in common with all others. They are all men, they are doers of good, they are all fictional characters, and they all have companions. Even the Lone Ranger had Tonto. The super heroes we have all grown up with have served an important role in men's development. It does not seem to matter whether as a dad you remember the Green Hornet, or as a son you remember the Power Ranger. These fictional characters have helped us focus on the "fight for law and order in the early west, or truth, justice, and the American way" in the Metropolis of our world. The most powerful role these super heroes have played, however, has been to fulfill our need for images and models. Every man needs a mentor, a membership in the club of other men, and a friend. I submit that in each of these roles, only a man will do. Women cannot fill these specific needs. Fact is, men need men.

The need for a mentor is so universally profound as to be the background and basis for the myth in Homer's Odessy. Men need mentors in every walk of life, in business as well as in the Christian community. Every man needs a mentor. God knew this, and supplied a dad for every lad. Unfortunately, many fathers today do not take their role seriously enough. Sons are abandoned, if not physically then emotionally. Boys are cheated out of the visual contact they need. Every son needs dad to help him get through life. In this program, you have a mentor. You are almost finished with the program itself, but you will never be finished with the need you have for dad in your life. Even when you are old and dad is gone, you will have the memory of his hand on your shoulder, sometimes heavy, sometimes gentle, directing you. His voice will be in your heart, and his words of wisdom will be in your ears, guiding you along.

The following description of how a dad progresses through life was handed to me at one of my Father's Conferences a few years ago. I found this unknown author's wisdom more than amusing. I think you will too.

How Fathers Mature

4	years:	My Daddy can do anything.
7	years:	My Dad knows a whole lot.
9	years:	Dad doesn't know quite everything.
12	years:	Dad just doesn't understand.
14	years:	Dad is old fashioned.
21	years:	That man is out of touch.
25	years:	Dad's okay.
30	years:	I wonder what Dad thinks about this.
35	years:	I must get Dad's input first.
50	years:	What would Dad have thought about that?
60	years:	I wish I could talk it over with Dad once more.

This may seem strange, but you will find it very fulfilling and cleansing. When the two of you are alone for this relational Milestone, try this unusual, but powerfully effective contact game. Get down on your knees facing each other. Each of you raise your hands up head-high, palms facing out toward the other. Touch the palms of your hands together, but do not interlock your fingers. Just set there on your knees, palms touching and look each other in the eyes. Speak silently with your mind. Father: "I love you, son." Son: "I love you Dad." Do this over and over and over without saying a word out loud. Stay on your knees in this position, speaking silently for several minutes. Don't worry about the time, or about anything else. Concentrate on your relationship as father and son. Each of you will know what the other is "saying" but no sound is coming out of your mouth. You are speaking with your eyes. No one else in the world will see you doing this, so you won't be embarrassed.

Notice some things about this humbling game. First, see how hard it was for dad to put himself in the same position as his son. See how hard is was for son to square off with his own dad. See how equalizing it was to get emotional. See how powerfully bonding it was to say I love you using only your eyes. In the next and final module, you will do this again, but then you will take it one step further. You'll see. Now, however, talk about this. Ask each other what the experience has done to your relationship. As you finish this session the point you should take with you is that it is time for dad to begin to acknowledge son as a man, in the world of other men. As a young man, it is time for you to begin to see life from your dad's eyes, in the world of older men. This is a world where men work. Men are responsible. Men are tough. Men are cruel. Men are obscene and indifferent. Men are dishonest, angry, ugly. They are competitive, cutting you off at every merging freeway, putting you down at every sports event. It is a world of men. But it is a world you must learn to live in. You cannot change your world, you cannot change other men. But you can begin to think like an adult man, in a world of other adult men. You will need help doing that. Dad is here. He always will be.

The Spiritual Question

This next-to-last Milestone is about how to stay accountable for the promises and commitments you have made as a man. It continues the above relational outing with dad by talking through the idea of friendship.

Let us look into the Word of God for a model of a good friendship. There is no better model than David and Jonathan (1 Samuel 18:1-4).

To kick off your discussion about this relationship, let me make a few brief comments about this relationship. First, it illustrates the way men can and should have a soul brother. Second, it gives men of every era the right to establish a friendship with other men. If David thought it a positive thing, then who are we to question God's model? Third, there was nothing unmanly about this relationship. The word used in this passage, translated "love," was a term used in covenant writings for agreement. It meant loyalty and bonding between two parties who would depend on each other for the fulfillment of their mutual contract.

In v. 4, Jonathan gave his garments and his weapons to David. This practice was common in those days, indicating that their transaction was complete. It seems obvious that Jonathan somehow knew that God had chosen David to be Israel's king, early in their friendship. Using this symbolic transfer of his belongings Jonathan demonstrated his own submission to God's will (See also 1 Samuel 20:30).

Male companions, close buddies. I hope you will read the book by Stu Weber, *Locking Arms*.[1] There is no better guide I know of to help us men face the issue of choosing and maintaining good male relationships. The way Stu suggests that we stay accountable is that we have at least one other bud with whom we can be ourselves. You need man friends, but more than that you need the close personal friendship of one other guy. Howard Hendricks told a stadium full of men at a Promise Keeper® Men's Conference in Boulder, Colorado, "You need a Barnabas, a buddy...who is not impressed with you..."[2] We need a friend we can't snow. Some guy who will look us in the eye and see our heart. He always knows when we are holding something back. He will always tell us the truth, and he is a guy who will go to the wall with us. Yep, the way to keep accountable is to have a friend and be a friend.

CHAPTER 20

MILESTONE 12

Expectations and Realities

Congratulations, you have come to the last Milestone. When this (and all other) Milestone has been checked off, you will be ready for your rite of passage ceremony. I hope this journey has been the experience you wanted it to be. I am sure it was not exactly what you expected. I never is. Other men have felt the same way. We enter this program with some expectations that never get fulfilled, sometimes because those expectations were unrealistic, sometimes because others let us down.

I may be speaking directly to a dad who has not been very serious about leading your son through all these milestones. Or I might be speaking to a son, who although you have 'completed the program' you have not actually cooperated emotionally. Or maybe I am speaking to a father-son team who have developed a really strong bond during these relational times together. Whatever the case, the time has come to move beyond the relational portion of this specific program into your public ceremony. In preparation for that, there is one more emotional game I ask you to play. Be sure you give plenty of time for this activity, and be sure you are alone.

Get into the position you were in Milestone 11, on your knees facing each other with your palms touching. Now interlock your fingers and actually lean on one another. The idea is to lean inward so that if the other person were not there you would fall forward. Put your full weight on the other person, but do not push. While in this position, leaning on each other, father welcomes son into the kingdom of adult men. Dad, look deeply into your son's eyes and into his soul. Tell him that you accept him as a man. Whatever else you need to say to him, do so. But do not miss this opportunity to invite your son to come into full manhood. Promise him your help and guidance, but not your interference. Promise him that you will always be there for him.

The only response from son is "Thank you, dad." Do not try to impress your dad with any words at this time. Let him do this as a gift to you. It is your private ritual. Later, in the ManTracks ceremony, you can have opportunity to thank him as you give your speech, but for now, let silence speak. Let the words of acceptance be absorbed. Allow the flow of Dad's love and spirit to move through your being as though it were a real current flowing through his interlocking fingers into your body.

Some men will want to pray together when they are in this position. Some men have reported powerful experiences during this time. When you get up from this kneeling position, give each other a big manly hug and congratulate each other for completing these Milestones.

Check out the next chapter. You have much to do to get ready for your ceremony. As you write your speech for the ceremony, remember to acknowledge all those who have made your program possible. You are stepping over a never to be repeated threshold. Take a long look back at your childhood. I hope it has been a good childhood, but whether good or not, you will never be back. It is time to say good-bye to the things of boys and hello to the things of men. Don't worry. You can handle it. You are a man.

The Spiritual Question

The last spiritual question you will consider in this program is "What does God want of my life?" To answer that question for yourself, you and your father should have this one last study in ManTracks together. I suggest you look into the book, *Seven Promises of a Promise Keeper*[1] and find among the several excellent chapters one that you both can agree would be a good study for the two of you. Take it to your intimate place and dig in. You will find this book to be for you what it has been for thousands of men across this nation. An excellent tool for interpersonal discussion on the issues of manhood. I suggest you study through the entire book together. Not for this Milestone! But for a project for the two of you. How about inviting one other young man and one other older man. The four of you could make a great small group.

Let me offer this prayer for you as you complete your ManTracks journey. Perhaps one of you could read the prayer out loud as you end your study together:

"Dear Heavenly Father:

Thank you for the opportunity to respond to your holy spirit as he has lead and is leading us as men. Give us the strength and courage to be men in todays world, the world you have placed us in. Help us be faithful to your word and to your calling on our lives. We pray for one another. We ask that your grace may be manifested in our family, in our church, in our community, and in our relationship. We submit to your direction in our lives and ask for the ability to be strong, to be men of integrity, and to stand against evil wherever we find it, and for Truth wherever we are. We are your sons. We acknowledge you as our Father. Guide us as we go from here to do your will.

We pray these things in the name of Jesus Christ our Lord.

Amen."

PART III

The ManTracks Rite of Passage Ceremony

CHAPTER 21

Preparation for the Rite of Passage Ceremony

Now that you have completed all your ManTracks Milestones, checked off all your activities and transferred all your journal entries, pictures and other momentos into your ManTracks Digest Album, you are ready to have your ceremony. The check list at the end of this chapter will help you get ready for that great day.

Setting The Date

The first thing you should do (you should have done this when you began Milestone 10), is set a date for your ceremony if you have not already done so. Everything below depends on that date. People need to be notified and informed in order to participate in your ceremony. Invitations to guest should be sent out at least six weeks ahead of time. An advisor should be chosen. Your pastor, or someone who has completed a ManTracks Ceremony before would be your best choices for this assignment. If you do not know anyone, please call the ManTracks

Seminar office phone number listed in the back of this book. Our ManTracks Staff will be happy to return your call and help you select someone in your area who would be a good advisor to help you with this important event. There is no charge for this service.

One important thing to remember about setting the date for your ManTracks rite-of-passage ceremony is that this ceremony will be a strange event to many people you want to invite. Your relatives and friends will think it is a nice idea, but since most of them have never seen anything like this, you cannot expect them to be as enthusiastic about it as you are. You have to tell them what you want them to do. This means giving plenty of time for people to get the ceremony plugged into their busy schedules. Don't set the date to compete with a major holiday, or on the same day many of your friends might be involved in other planned events. Of course, it is impossible to set the date by everyone else's calendar, but try not to compete with things that will make attendance difficult for the majority of your friends and family.

Another thing you must decide is the day of the week you want to have your ceremony. Do you want it to be in the afternoon of the day your church has its regular worship? Should it be at night? You must decide, but it would be a good thing to check with your church office for clues of the best time. The person who keeps the master calendar for all your church's events will be able to help. Again, give plenty of time for planning ahead. Our suggestion is to plan the date at least three months in advance.

Ordering and Mailing Invitations

Naturally, the deadline for ordering your invitations depends on the date you have set for your ceremony. The thing to remember here is that your invitations are the only way some folks will know what you are doing. A sample invitation in the appendix will give you an idea of how to word your invitation, however, do not be tied to my sample. Use your own ideas and make this as personal as you wish it to be. It is after all a one-time event for you. Create it any way you like.

Planning the Ceremony

I have outlined a ManTracks Ceremony agenda that has worked well for many folks over the years. You will find a detailed example in the appendix. Here again, you are encouraged to create your own. The idea of the ceremony, remember, is to celebrate the coming of age of a young Christian man. The most important part of the ceremony is the Father's Blessing. You will find several examples of the Father's Blessing in the Appendix. If the wording is not suitable for your situation, change it. The main idea is to tell the son in a formal, public way, that his father now pronounces manhood upon him. I cannot emphasize this enough. This is what the entire ManTracks program is about. If this one factor fails to be projected, the entire program has failed.

The Master Of Ceremonies

A Master of Ceremonies, as chosen by the son, welcomes attendees and explains the procedures of the ManTracks program. He or she reviews the process that has occurred during the past few months as the host father and son have participated in the ManTracks Milestones. The format can differ, of course, as the host family desires. For instance, in Raymond's (our third son) ceremony, the Master of Ceremonies introduced a third person to outline the ManTracks program. Also, both older brothers, who had experienced ManTracks for themselves, were on the program. Early on, someone leads the congregation in an invocation prayer. The people selected to carry out the various functions can be family members, friends or anyone the son being honored wishes.

Music

The service includes musical arrangements as prescribed by the ManTracks family. Solo's or duets, etc., are appropriate. The type and amount of music is up to the planners. The program should not be solemn, it should be upbeat and cheerful, with a positive flavor. We want our sons to be honored, and we want to design and carry the program out in such a way as to make it an outstanding punctuation mark in the ManTracks candidate's future. For this reason, contemporary music may be the right choice.

Photographs

The ceremony, like a wedding, includes pictures. Since photographs are a significant part of the ManTracks memoirs, photographs should be taken of each part of the ceremony. Often, the entire process is video taped. One of the underlying motivations of your ceremony is to interest other families in the process.

The Pastoral Charge

The ManTracks family minister, or some other person who understands the ManTracks biblical base, is requested to present a "pastoral charge" intended to challenge the son, the father and the family. The preacher is responsible for giving the biblical background and basis for such a program. This includes a sermon on the responsibility of being a Christian adult male. I recall at one of our son's ceremony, the pastor brought to life the Greco-Roman practice of "Paidagogeia." This was the process of bringing a Greek free-man to maturity. A well trusted salve was given mentor duty over the developing son of his master. The slave, whose title was Paidogogs, had the responsibility to get the young man to school and back home safely. Moreover, the Paidagogs saw to it that the lad study and participate in "manly" things.

You can see the ideal analogy for ManTracks. Another pastoral charge I remember was based on Ecclesiastes 12:1-7, where the minister reminded the young man to remember his Creator while he was young. Another message to the son being charged with manhood was from 1 Timothy 4:12 *"Do not let anyone make light of your youthful position, rather be an example of masculine behavior."* Just give your minister the opportunity. He will come up with the appropriate biblical text for your ManTracks ceremony. It would be a good thing if you asked him and all participants to read this book so as to be more prepared to help you put on a good program.

The Passage Statement

A main highlight of the ManTracks ceremony is a "Passage Statement" read by the father or by another male relative, such as a an older brother, a grandfather or an uncle.

The following "Passage Statement" has been used several times in ManTracks ceremonies:

"We have gathered today to pay tribute to _____ who has completed his requirements for a formal "Rite-of-Passage" program called ManTracks. During the past several months, _____ and his dad have met consistently and discussed the attitudes and characteristics of an adult Christian man. They have concentrated

177

on three areas of _____'s development, Spiritual, emotional and relational. In the Spiritual area, _____ has acknowledged a personal relationship with God as the perfect father, and has attempted to model Jesus Christ, who is the perfect son. Emotionally, _____ has confronted psychological and social issues pertinent to adult manhood, and masculine behavior. In the Relational aspect of his program, _____ and his dad have concentrated on their intercommunication. They have spent a great deal of time with each other, which as you know—in the fast-paced world we live in— is a precious commodity. During this period, _____ and _____ have completed twelve milestones, or guide lines for male maturity. _____ is ready to put his childhood behind him and step into the world of Christian manhood. This ceremony will help him do that."

If appropriate, an older brother or a close friend could acknowledge the son's passage into manhood (like a brief testimony) after the Passage Statement has been read. When this is done, it really adds flavor to the service. In our own case, Jim participated in both his brothers' ceremonies. Jim and Mark participated in Raymond's program. The content of the testimony usually follows the idea that the brother, friend, uncle (or whoever is giving the testimony) tells of his personal relationship with the ManTracks son. They tell a story or give evidence that he has developed maturity and integrity in his personal and private affairs, as well as taking more and more responsibility in an adult world.

The Son Being Honored Gives A Speech

The son's speech is one of the main high points of the ceremony. It is a short statement of realization and a verbal acceptance of the responsibilities of adult manhood, as outlined by the minister. The speech includes at least three elements: (a) A statement of Christian faith. This is a public acknowledgment that the *ManTracks* son has made a conscious, adult decision to follow the teachings of Jesus Christ; that he has a family relationship with the body of Christ, and that he is accepting the responsibilities of adult Christian manhood. (b) He acknowledges that he is not yet fully grown, that he has more growing to do; but that he is old enough to understand the need for a rite of passage, and he desires to be recognized as an adult and be judged as such. Finally, he presents himself as a responsible person who can be depended upon to carry the gospel of Jesus Christ into the next generation, to support and defend the Christian faith and the traditions of historic Christianity, and to act in a responsible way in his public and private life. He ends his speech by asking the congregation to witness his father's blessing.

In addition the lad acknowledges his father's role in their relationship and program, giving his father a public "verbal" 'hug' or thank-you. He acknowledges and thanks his mother as well.

The Reception

The reception following the ManTracks ceremony resembles a wedding reception. It includes refreshments and a formal receiving line for the father and the son to greet attendees and well-wishers. In all our ceremonies, the ManTracks mom took the responsibility for this important occasion, however, in most cases other parents and family friends participated also. The person in charge of the reception solicits other relatives and friends to assist in making this reception a meaningful memory. Photographs and other memoirs of the milestone period are displayed at the reception. Music is appropriate, and a guest-book is presented for all attendees to register their attendance. The contents of the guest register becomes a permanent part of the ManTracks Digest (album).

Final Preparation For ManTracks Rite Of Passage Ceremony

❏ All Twelve Milestones Have Been Checked Off

❏ All Memoirs Have Been Inserted Into Our Digest

❏ Mom's Check-Off List Is Requested

❏ Final Appointment With Advisor Is Scheduled

❏ Date Set For Ceremony_____

❏ Invitations Sent

❏ Program Planned

❏ All Participants Designated

❏ "Pastoral Charge" minister selected, his invitation accepted

❏ Son's Speech Is Written

❏ Son Has Practiced His Speech

❏ "Father's Blessing" Ready

❏ "Passage Statement" Prepared

❏ Advisor's Sign-off

❏ Flowers Ordered

❏ Decorations and Reception People Ready To Prepare Reception

❏ Day of Ceremony "Last-minute-items" check off

_____

_____

_____

_____

CHAPTER 22

The ManTracks Rite of Passage Ceremony

Most people will want their rite of passage program to be conducted similar to a church service. It is, after all a ceremony emphasizing the son's coming of age as a Christian man. If you wish your service to be like the ones we have suggested in this book, then one thing to settle on is the music that will be a part of the ceremony. Music can make the program go much nicer, especially if soothing instrumental music is played as guests arrive. But do keep it upbeat, warm and cheerful. Guests are seated by ushers, who should be friends and peers of the son being honored. Special seating arrangements are made for grandparents and immediate family members. Someone recommended that grandparents be included in the ceremony during the pronouncement of the father's Blessing. That turned out to be a good idea. Grandparents seem to appreciate what ManTracks means to the family heritage. Often, their presence adds depth and character to the ceremony.

A Suggested Order Of Service For The ManTracks Ceremony

Prelude . . . . .Music while ushers seat guests:
(Participants sit on front row—Grandparents and other relatives sit on
second row. All other guests are seated as designated by the family).

Music . . . .(solo, duet, etc.)

Welcome . . . . .M.C. (explanation of the
ceremony...)

Invocation by MC, or MC introduces the person designated by
family to pray.

Congregational Singing . . . . . . .This option may include a music
leader, as the family desires.

Statement of Purpose . . . . .ManTracks Father (or some other
family member).

Acknowledgment . . . . .A big brother, relative, or friend,
(Someone who is known to have personal knowledge of the
ManTracks son, offers a testimony that the ManTracks candidate is
ready for this manhood passage).

"Passage Request" . . . . .ManTracks son gives a speech,
requesting recognition as a
Christian man.

Pastoral Charge . . . . .Minister (Family pastor, or
invited guest preacher offers a
Biblical charge toward godly
manhood).

Father's Blessing . . . . .Father and son stand before the
congregation as father puts his
hands on head or shoulders of
son and blesses him for manhood.

Closing . . . . .Prayer and or song.

Reception

The climax of the ceremony is the "Father's Blessing." The father places his hands on the son's shoulders as they both face the audience, and pronounces the Blessing. This is sometimes accompanied by the father passing to his son an item of remembrance, some token of personal value. I gave my son Raymond a pocket knife that my grandfather gave me. Mark, my step-son whose father was killed in an airplane crash, was presented with his father's Bible. The service ends when the father presents his son to the congregation as a man. The following blessings are typical of the wording of the ManTracks ceremony:

The Father's Blessing

1. For a biological son

"This is my son __(name)_____. When he was a baby I held him in my arms and had a thousand dreams for him. As he grew, I saw the unique expression of God's grace and [a positive character trait - one of his major strengths] developing in him. For the past [six] months we have labored to address some of the issues he is confronting and will confront throughout his life as a man. I present to you a man: _____ my son in whom I am well pleased. I publicly acknowledge and affirm his manhood. He has successfully navigated this rite of passage, it is now up to him to live the part. I lay my hand of blessing and affirmation upon you, and in the name of Jesus Christ I say: 'and now you are a man, my son.'"

2. "Today is a special day. Jim, you are not really grown yet, but you are no longer a boy. By this event, you are being welcomed into the kingdom of men. The time has come to recognize your adult manhood... So, before God Almighty, maker of heaven and earth, the One who created you man, I pronounce your coming of age as a man. From this time forward, wherever you go, hold your head erect and your shoulders high. You are a man. You have entered the realm of male adults, and you are now responsible to accept as your own the challenge from First Corinthians, chapter sixteen and verse thirteen and fourteen: 'Be on your guard; stand firm in the faith; be [a

man] of courage; be strong. Whatever you do, do in love.' Jim, It is my distinct pleasure to pronounce to the world that you are my son in whom I am well pleased. Even as you receive my blessing, I let the world know that now you are a man, my son."

3. For a foster, adopted or step-son

"This is __(name)_____ I have watched him grow and loved him as a father. His (character strength)   has blessed our home. I was blessed when became a part of my life. We have shared a common home, a common family, and a common Lord these   Number years. Now over the past six months, he has entered into the ManTracks rite of passage and successfully completed its requirements. I witness before you his coming of age. I lay my hands on you, _____, and give you my blessing and my affirmation. I say, on your behalf, before God and these assembled witnesses, 'And now you are a man, my son.'"

4. General

__(name)_____, because of your successful completion of the ManTracks rite of passage program, and because you have shown the characteristic evidences of coming of age, and of maturity as a man, I pronounce on you my blessing: Laying my hands on you, in the name of Jesus Christ, I pray that you may know the presence and power of God in the fellowship of other men, for you are now a man, my son."

CHAPTER 23

A Final word

Frequently Asked Questions

The following questions are asked almost everywhere I introduce the ManTracks program. My responses represent a disclaimer as well as a means of satisfying the inquirer's request for information. Common sense tells us that ManTracks isn't for everyone. Some father-son teams will never function well in this type of program. The reasons are as varied as the people to whom I have presented the Mantracks material. I have found the greatest amount of problems among people who have blown past my caution signs, and taken the program on despite the obvious warning labels. I will begin with the most commonly asked questions first, and deal with the rare situations last.

Could I Take My Step-sons Through ManTracks?

Most step-sons need this program even more than biological youth because there exists a likely possibility that the step-son feels abandoned by his biological dad. This is true even if the step-son's biological father is nearby. There may be evidence of passive aggression, or the fear of future rejection by the step-father. These problems do not need to be overcome before beginning ManTracks because a strong bond will usually result in the process of this program.

A few guidelines for step-fathers who wish to bring their step-sons through ManTracks should be considered.

First, the step-son must be in full agreement. After he has an opportunity to review this book, work through the questions following chapters 1-4. If both of you wish to work the program, then by all means begin. If, on the other hand, one of you feels reluctance, discuss the issues that stand between you and working on a rite of passage together. The young man must be free to express his feelings and make his own conscious choice about the program without pressure from anyone.

Next, the step-son's mother must be in full agreement with the program. Don't just tell her you are going to take her son through a bonding experience that will result in a Christian rite of passage ceremony. Your step-son's mother is a very important part of the Emotional Development section of some of the Milestones. She must agree with the process, and she must really want the results for her son. If she does not, I urge you to abandon the project until you can get into Christian counseling with her to resolve the issues that stand between you and her son.

Finally, your step-son's biological father should be given the opportunity to consent to the program. I realize this is a bold suggestion. Every situation is different, and of course there are several situations that make talking to the biological father impractical. However if there is even the slightest possibility of a rational conversation, then I urge you to try to discuss the ManTracks program with the biological dad. Many issues enter into making you the key modeling figure in your step-son's life. It may be that your situation is too soon, or relationships may be too hostile. If this is the case, the better part of wisdom is to wait a year or so while you pray for the relationship between your step-son and you to become mature enough for you to play the lead role in the ManTracks program.

If you do get to talk to your son's biological father, consider the conversation one man, Bill had with his step-son's biological father asking permission to take Tim through a rite of passage program. After four months of praying about it, and discussing the issue with Tim's mother, Bill made an appointment with Tim's biological father. He probably thought Bill wanted to talk about visitation rights or the back child support he had never paid, so he was a little defensive at first. Bill assured him that what he wanted to discuss was rather unusual and it ought to be discussed face-to-face, but that it wasn't anything bad. He gave bill the appointment.

"I am really glad I have an opportunity to help you raise Tim." Bill began, after very little small talk. "He is developing into a fine young man and I have grown to really love him. I want you to know right up front that I desire only the best for Tim. You can always count on me to look after his best interests. I'd like your permission to be Tim's guide through a rite of passage program. Can I tell you about it?

"Sure," he said. "Go ahead."

"You know, —[name withheld]—, when you and I were growing up, we didn't have anything like this to help us identify a point in time when we became a man. This program is a six-month training program that focuses on Tim's responsibilities as an adult male. It helps him confront such issues as integrity, honor, dependability, sexuality, and career path discovery. I think it will be of great value to him as he starts to mature as a man. But because I do not want you to think I am trying to usurp your authority as his biological father, I would appreciate your approval. Would it be all right with you if I sign Tim up for this program?

[_____] asked Bill a few questions about what the program cost and seemed genuinely interested until Bill brought up the Christian perspective. He wasn't very keen on religion, but he seemed to respect Bill's courtesy and he responded positively to the respect Bill showed him man-to-man. He gave his permission, and that was that. He never asked another question, and he did not come to the ceremony when sent an invitation.

What if the biological father is gone?

For those fathers who live with sons whose natural father is not available (death, true abandonment, etc.) the situation is a little different. You should have a much greater chance of success with the ManTracks program than dads who must deal with a jealous biological father every other week-end. You should assume "fatherhood" and follow the guidelines as though the young man in the program with you is your biological offspring.

Why Only Boys, Why Not Have a Rite Of Passage Program for Girls?

I have been in communication with a group of godly parents who are my very good friends. They have conducted a female version of rite of passaage which they call a "Passage Tea" for several daughters last summer. I have also heard of other programs that offer a coming-of-age party, or ceremony for young ladies. I will begin the first steps of a program for young women in the near future.

Another answer to the question, however, is that men are the responsible parties in the Christian community. Most evangelical Christian leaders agree that when a man gets his head on straight, women respect and admire his attempts at leadership. As we work on getting young men committed to their Christian leadership responsibilities, we will see obvious changes in their vital relationships. The next generation will not seek their esteem in the world. They will have a godly dad to give them the competence they need.

What Minimum Age Should A Son Be For the ManTracks Program To Be Effective?

Naturally, age is not the main factor, maturity is. ManTracks cannot make you mature, but it certainly will reveal whether you are maturing. Almost anyone who can comprehend what they read could 'go through' the program. However, it is not filling in the blanks and completing the projects that make the difference. It is a relationship that is developed between a young man and his father that causes the unique changes that occur during the program. Unless the young man really understands some of life's mysteries, he will be overwhelmed with the program. I have seen several good exceptions to the rule, but usually ages 15-17 make the best candidates. Again, this depends on the individual situation that exists between the young man and his dad.

Can the ManTracks Program Be a Group Project?

It definitely can be a group of several fathers and sons participating together. This increases the interest level, especially among the young men. I recommend a group of three to ten. More than ten becomes hard to manage. I have found it successful to meet once per month and share in a group how everyone is doing with their individual programs. I do not recommend that everyone attempt to progress at the same pace, but in a group, this seems best. Some dad-son teams can move faster through the projects than others. The main thing with groups is the comradeship and accountability it gives. A group should choose a leader to guide them, a pastor or church elder would be a good choice, especially if he has adult children. Although he never went through the ManTracks program, the principles in it are very familiar to most evangelical Christian leaders.

This Seems Like A Great Program To Take To Street Kids Who Have No Dad At Home. Do You See ManTracks As An Evangelistic Tool?

It may seem that way, but it is not an evangelistic tool. ManTracks will not be successful with a situation where there is no lasting, long-term relationship between father and son. The program was designed with the last verse of the Old Testament in mind. This program is intended to turn the hearts of the fathers to the sons and the hearts of the sons to the father. The resulting relationship will give the son confidence, competence, self-esteem and a model for how to live the Christian life as a responsible male adult. This is not to say that bonding could not occur with a non-family relationship. Certainly the possibility exists, but the situation would probably only succeed if the street youth took up residence in the home of the older male adult. It is in the context of the daily routine of home and family that we learn our basics and decide who we are and whose we are. The process of life is not managed through a weekly program. It is a day by day learning experience, and the home is the institution God designed for life-transference to occur.

APPENDIX

"PAI CHARIS"

In almost every culture there is a ceremony that marks a point in time when a boy becomes a man. In American society an illustration of this is the Jewish "Bar Mitzvah." The "Pai Charis" [which is Greek for "child of Grace"] seems an appropriate ceremony for the Christian boy. "Pai Charis" will celebrate the young Christian's entrance into manhood and will be a means of charging him with his responsibilities.

Mr. and Mrs. Ellis A. Hackler, Jr.
warmly invite you to attend
"Pai Charis"
to celebrate the fourteenth birthday of their son, Jim,
Friday, August, twenty-sixth, seven thirty p.m.
Northside Baptist Church in Irving.
Reception following ceremony in Fellowship Hall.
R.S.V.P.   283-0473

Endnotes

Chapter 1

1. Minirth, Frank, Brian Newman, and Paul Warren. The Father Book, 1992, Nashville: Thomas Nelson Publishers, p.187-188.

2. The original name of our coming-of-age program was "Pai-Charis." The name was changed to **ManTracks** because the original name seemed to difficult for marketing to the general public. However, the original term carried a strong symbolic meaning, and I gave it up reluctantly. I used two Greek words Pai, represented **Paideuo** [to train, or instruct], **Paidagogos** [the attendant or guide, who was training a young boy in school], **Paidea** the process of discipleship, and **Pais**, a young male, and **Charis** meaning grace. The new term, **Pai-Charis** means "One being trained by (in) grace" For a more exhaustive study, validating the biblical basis for a rite of passage program, such as the one I have designed, see Munce, William D. The Analytical Lexicon To The Greek New Testament, 1993, Grand Rapids: Zondervan Publishing House, p.348; and Bromiley, Goffrey W. The Theological Dictionary of the New Testament [Little Kittel], 1985, Grand Rapids: William B. Eerdmans Publishing Company, pp 753-758. The name **Pai-Charis**, copyright © 1976, was used for our 'coming of age' program until the program name was changed to ManTracks©, 1995.

3. Captain John F. Baldwin, CHC, USN. Keynote speaker at the Baccalaureate Breakfast in honor of Officer Candidate Class 87006, United States Navy, Naval Officer Candidate School, Naval Education and Training Center, Newport, RI, 19 November, 1987.

Chapter 2

1. The sample invitation, shown in the Appendix is a photo copy of the actual invitation we first used, thus the name "Pai-Charis."

Chapter 3

1. Horn Creek Christian Family Camp, West Cliff, Colorado, is one of the most relaxing and enjoyable family camps I have ever visited. It is located in the Sangria De Christi mountains of central Colorado, about sixty miles north of Pueblo. Good luck trying to get

in, many families re-book for the next year after every stay, and there is a long waiting list. Some family and church groups have been going there every year for decades. Deanna and I took our three boys and escaped to Horn Creek the first week in June for eight years. Some of our family's fondest memories occurred on those trips.

2. Bly, Robert. Iron John, 1992, New York: Vintage Books, pp. ix.

3. Weber, Stu, Locking Arms, 1995, Sisters: Questar Publishers, Inc., p.248.

Chapter 4

1. My son, Raymond was born in 1968. It would have been good if I had experienced some father love as a child so that I would have known how to sacrifice my own personal desires for my son's future. When his mom and I divorced, I experienced an emotional crisis. By the time I had completed my 'recovery' under the competent counsel of Dr. James Kitchens, Ph.D., and the healing grace of Jesus Christ, I had remarried. My new wife, Deanna had two sons. Jim, then nine years old, was the product of a broken home when he was an infant; and Mark, age four, was the product of a marriage interrupted by his father's death in an airplane crash. I now had three boys in my home. I was dad to three fellows who each had different biological fathers. Jim, age 9, Mark, age 4, and Ray, age 4. God got my attention and I began to make up for lost time, trying to be a good dad. The hardest lesson any step-dad has to learn is that God is a forgiving God. He wants us to mend our fences, put the past behind us, and live by His standards. I once heard Billy Graham say, "You can't unscramble eggs." You can reconcile, however. Even if former relationships cannot be restored, conflicts can be resolved. I know. My ex-wife Sandra will agree that the past is over and the future is in God's hands. I encourage every man who has experienced this awful social chasm to resolve all conflicts and go on with their lives. Maybe you can see why, in my counseling practice, I specialize in helping to repair broken homes.

2. The New Testament is chucked full of the emphasis God places on relationships. To kick-start your thinking about this, consider John 13:33. How can we love someone if we do not have a relationship with them? See 1 John 1:3-7. The word fellowship (as in Hebrews 10:24-25) is the most commonly used term in the New Testament for the idea of relationships. Koinonia is nothing less than

reciprocal living. It takes relationship to behave like Christians. Building relationships that honor God's idea of family, church, and community, is just about the most important thing on earth.

Chapter 5

1. These names are not real, but the people are, and so are their stories. In my role as Christian Counselor, I have been privileged to listen to men and women tell stories like these for more than twenty years, but I never got used to it. It continues to break my heart to hear the horror stories of people who have been reared in dysfunctional homes, experienced father-abandonment, violence and sexual abuse. What child is born immune to the need for both parents? Family is a team sport. My heart goes out to every single parent in the world, because their children are among the most vulnerable. Obviously, the parent who stays by the child and does her or his best to be a good parent under the circumstances they have been handed, deserves our prayers and our support. But the point I am making cannot be rejected as insignificant: Without dads in their life on a constant basis, just as God designed, every child will have a father wound. That wound cannot be healed by society, the church, Parents Without Partners, Twelve-Steps, Boy Scouts, Girl Scouts, or any other well-meaning program. Those programs are good as far as they go, and they can help, but only God can heal the father wound. I have seen many, many people broken and ruined before they tried his cure. Sad!

2. I adopted these ten commandments from a list I found in a study guide written by Brian Wallace and Cindy Bunch, in a 1993 InterVarsity Press publication, called "Created Male & Female Bible Studies." The list was in the 'Created Male study,' page 1. Although the list was not in the "10 Commandment" form I framed it in, the core list is close enough to be considered their idea. I added the names Mascule and Femina and made other changes.

3. Cranfield, Ken. National Center For Fathering. Survey published in Today's Father, February, 1995.

4. An advertising brochure, telling the value of the National Center For Fathering, posted these data, citing the survey noted above.

5. Pittman, Frank S. III, Man Enough: Fathers, Sons, and the Search for Masculinity, 1993, New York: G. P. Putnam's Sons Publishers, p.115

Chapter 6

1. I Got the baseball analogy from Larry Parker, President of Promise University, when we were relaxing by the fire in a cabin at Brotherhood Camp, near Bremerton, Washington, February, 1995. I told Larry I was going to try it in my book, and give him credit. So if it sounds dumb—talk to Larry. His national conferences on fathering have blessed many. You can contact him to get on his mailing list, order resources that help dads do their stuff, or find out about his seminars at Promise University, 1230 NE Brockman Pl., Seattle, WA 98125. Ph. 1-800-669-7972.

Chapter 7

1. Each of these quotes appeared in a different television program. I admit they were pure humor, in the context of situation comedy programs or stand-up comedy acts. In their original genre, none of them were intended as political statements. Not directly, anyhow. Yet doesn't it strike you as odd that you are hard-pressed to find a 'sit-com' that does not put men in a bafoon, irresponsible, clown-type role? Take my challenge: channel-surf yourself to death, find one program produced after 1990, and aired on any major TV network, that casts the leading men in responsible roles of integrity. Where are the TV programs that magnify men as, mentally sound, emotionally stable, competent husbands and wise fathers?

2. Larry Parker gets credit for this story, too. We told each other a lot of stories during that male-bonding night. I wonder if I will ever read any of my yarns in his books?

3. The old hymn was a regular favorite at the Emanuel Baptist Church, in Pittsburg, Texas where my Grandpa Copeland was a Deacon. The song was written and arranged by Albert E. Brumley. It was hymn number 63 in the Heavenly Highway Hymns, Pangburn, AR: Stamps-Baxter Music & Printing Co., publication, 1956.

4. Hosea 8:7: "They sow the wind and reap the whirlwind. The stalk has no head; it will produce no flour. Were it to yield grain, foreigners would swallow it up." Sound familiar? Christians are facing a whirlwind of violence today, due to irresponsible, sowing-to-to-the-wind mentality of leaders in colleges, political and church offices in the 1960's and 1970's. When will we ever learn…?

Chapter 13

1. These data came from a report of the Best Insurance Rating Guide, copied in a New York Life Insurance Company brochure, published in 1995.

Chapter 16

1. Covey, Steven, Principle Centered Leadership, 1989. NY: Fireside/Simon and Schuster, Page 246.

2. Sanders, J. Oswald Spiritual Leadership, 1967. The Moody Bible Institute of Chicago, Page 20.

Chapter 18

1. Kegan, Robert The Evolving Self, Problems and Process in Human Development, 1982. Cambridge: Harvard University Press, p. 172.

2. Pittman, Frank S. Man Enough: Fathers, Sons, and The Search for Masculinity, 1993. New York: G. P. Putnam's Sons, Publishers.

Chapter 19

1. Weber, Stu Locking Arms: God's Design for Masculine Friendships, 1995. Sisters: Questar Publishers, Inc.

2. Howard Hendricks, speaking on Saturday morning at the 1993 Promise Keepers® Conference, Bolder Colorado.

Chapter 20

1. Seven Promises of a Promise Keeper, is editied by Al Janssen, Promise Keepers 1994, Colorado Springs: Focus On The Family Publishing.

Bibliography

Betetcher, R. William. *In A Time Of Fallen Heroes: The Recreation Of Masculinity,* 1993. New York: Atheneum Press.

Bly, Robert. *Iron John: A Book About Men,* 1992. New York: Vintage Books.

Covey, Steven. *Principle Centered Leadership,* 1991. New York: Fireside/Simon and & Schuster.

_____ *The Seven Habits of Highly Effective People,* 1987 New York: Fireside/Simon and & Schuster.

Crabb, Larry Jr. And Lawrence Crabb, Sr. *God of My Father: A Son's Reflections On His Father's Walk of Faith,* 1994. Grand Rapids: Zondervan Publishing House.

_____ Inside Out, 1988. Colorado Springs: NavPress.

Dalby, Gordon. *Father and Son—The Wound, The Healing, The call to Manhood,* 1992. Nashville: Thomas Nelson.

Davis, Phil. *The Father I never Knew,* 1991. Colorado Springs: NavPress.

Dobson, James. *Emotions, Can You Trust Them,* 1980. Ventura: Regal Books.

_____ *Turning Hearts Toward Home,* 1989. Dallas: Word Publishing.

_____ *Straight Talk To Men and Their Wives,* 1980. Waco: Word Books.

Druck, Ken. *The Secrets Men Keep,* 1985. Garden City: Doubleday.

Farmer, Steven. *The Wounded Male,* 1991. New York: Ballantine Books, Inc.

Farrar, Steve. *Point Man,* 1990. Sisters: Questar Publishers, Inc.

_____ *Standing Tall,* 1994. Sisters: Questar Publishers, Inc.

Garfinkel, Perry. *In A Man's World: Father, Son, Brother, Friend, and Other Roles Men Play,* 1992. Berkeley: Ten Speed Press

Goldberg, Herb. *The Inner Male: Overcoming Roadblocks To Intimacy,* 1987: New York: New American Library.

Grey, John. *Men Are from Mars, Women Are from Venus,* 1992. New York: Harper Collins Publishers.

Heidebrecht, Paul. *Time To Go Home: Turning the Hearts of Fathers to Their Children,* 1990. Norcross: Great Commission Publications.

Hicks, Robert. *Uneasy Manhood: The Quest For Self Understanding,* 1991. Nashville: Oliver Nelson Publishing.

_____. *The Masculine Journey: Understanding the Six Stages of Manhood,* 1993. Colorado Springs: NavPress Publishing Group.

Keen, Sam. *Fire In The Belly: On Being A Man,* 1991. New York: Bantam Books.

Kegan, Robert. *The Evolving Self: Problems and Process in Human Development,* 1982. Cambridge: Harvard University Press.

Kiley, Dan. *The Peter Pan Syndrome: Men Who Have Never Grown Up,* 1983. New York: Dodd, Mead.

Lee, John H. *At My Father's Wedding: Reclaiming Our True Masculinity,* 1991. New York: Bantam Books.

Mc Dowell, Josh. *His Image, My Image,* 1984. San Bernardino: Here's Life Publishers, Inc.

Mc Gee, Robert S. *The Search For Signifance,* 1990. Houston: Rapha Publishing.

Minirth, Frank, Brian Newman, and Paul Warren. *The Father Book: An Instruction Manual,* 1992. Nashville: Thomas Nelson Publishers.

Moore, Robert L. *The King Within: Accessing The Male Psyche,* 1992. New York: W. Morrow.

_____ *The Warrior Within: Accessing The Knight In The Male Psyche,* 1992. New York: W. Morrow.

_____ *The Magician Within: Assessing the Shaman In The Male Psyche,* 1992. New York: W. Morrow.

Morley, Pat. *The Man in the Mirror,* 1992. Nashville: Thomas Nelson, Inc.

Moyers, Bill. "A Gathering of Men" [video recording] Bill Moyers with Robert Bly. 1990. New York: Mystic Fire Video.

Murphey, Cecil. *ManTalk: Resources for Exploring Men's Issues*, 1991. Louisville: Presbyterian Publishing House.

Osherson, Samuel. *Finding Our Fathers*, 1986. New York: Free Press.

Pittman, Frank S. *Man Enough: Fathers, Sons, and The Search for Masculinity*, 1993. New York: G. P. Putnam's Sons, Publishers.

Promise Keepers. *Seven Promises of a Promise Keeper*, edited by Al Janssen. 1994. Colorado Springs: Focus On The Family Publishing.

Pruett, Kyle. *The Nurturing Father*, 1987. New York: Warner Books.

Ross, John Munder. *The Male Paradox*, 1992. New York: Simon & Schuster.

Sanders, J. Oswald. *Spiritual Leadership*, 1967, 1980, 1994. Second Revision: The Moody Bible Institute of Chicago.

Schreur, Jack and Jerry Schreur. *Fathers & Sons*, 1995. Wheaton: Victor Books.

Simmons, Dave. *Dad, The Family Coach*, 1991. Wheaton: Victor Books.

_____ *Dad, The Family Counselor*, 1991. Wheaton: Victor Books.

_____ *Dad, The Family Mentor*, 1992. Wheaton: Victor Books.

Smalley, Gary and John Trent. *The Blessing*, 1986. Nashville: Thomas Nelson.

_____ *The Hidden Value Of A Man*, 1992. Colorado Springs: Focus On The Family Publishing.

Swindoll Charles R. *Home, Where Life Makes Up Its Mind*, 1979. Portland: Multnomah Press.

Weber, Stu. *Tender Warrior*, 1993. Sisters: Questar Publishers, Inc.

_____ *Locking Arms: God's Design for Masculine Friendships*, 1995. Sisters: Questar Publishers, Inc.

Wilder, James. *Just Between Father and Son*, 1990. Downers Grove: Intervarsity Press.

Williams, Charles. *Forever A Father, Always A Son*, 1991. Wheaton: Victor Books.

To order additional copies of

ManTracks

please send $9.99
plus $3.95 shipping and handling to:

Ellis Hackler
3587 Town Square Dr.
San Jose, CA 95127

*Quantity Discounts are Available

To order by phone,
have your credit card ready and call
1-800-917-BOOK